D0568350

ace Sound

ic Projects

for All Ages

APR 1 6 2018

APR 1 6 2018

DISCARD

About the Authors

Mary L. Glendening is the Director of the Middletown Free Library in Media, Pennsylvania. She has been running maker programs at the library for several years. Mary is the author of *From Video Games to Real Life: Tapping into Minecraft to Inspire Creativity and Learning in the Library.*

Isaac W. Glendening is one-half of the band Cesium 137. He is a professional audio engineer and owner of Subversive Sound Studio. Isaac introduces kids and teens to the wonders of audio through iPad apps, soft synths, and littleBits.

DISCARD

Makerspace Sound and Music Projects for All Ages

Mary L. Glendening

Isaac W. Glendening

New York   Chicago   San Francisco
Athens   London   Madrid
Mexico City   Milan   New Delhi
Singapore   Sydney   Toronto

Library of Congress Control Number: 2017957634

McGraw-Hill Education books are available at special quantity discounts to use as premiums and sales promotions or for use in corporate training programs. To contact a representative, please visit the Contact Us page at www.mhprofessional.com.

Makerspace Sound and Music Projects for All Ages

Copyright © 2018 by McGraw-Hill Education. All rights reserved. Printed in the United States of America. Except as permitted under the United States Copyright Act of 1976, no part of this publication may be reproduced or distributed in any form or by any means, or stored in a database or retrieval system, without the prior written permission of the publisher.

1 2 3 4 5 6 7 8 9   LOV   22 21 20 19 18 17

ISBN   978-1-260-02707-5
MHID   1-260-02707-4

This book is printed on acid-free paper.

Sponsoring Editor Michael McCabe	**Proofreader** Claire Splan
Editing Supervisor Stephen M. Smith	**Indexer** Claire Splan
Production Supervisor Pamela A. Pelton	**Art Director, Cover** Jeff Weeks
Project Manager Patricia Wallenburg, TypeWriting	**Composition** TypeWriting
Copy Editor James K. Madru	

McGraw-Hill Education, the McGraw-Hill Education logo, TAB, and related trade dress are trademarks or registered trademarks of McGraw-Hill Education and/or its affiliates in the United States and other countries and may not be used without written permission. All other trademarks are the property of their respective owners. McGraw-Hill Education is not associated with any product or vendor mentioned in this book.

Information contained in this work has been obtained by McGraw-Hill Education from sources believed to be reliable. However, neither McGraw-Hill Education nor its authors guarantee the accuracy or completeness of any information published herein, and neither McGraw-Hill Education nor its authors shall be responsible for any errors, omissions, or damages arising out of use of this information. This work is published with the understanding that McGraw-Hill Education and its authors are supplying information but are not attempting to render engineering or other professional services. If such services are required, the assistance of an appropriate professional should be sought.

We would like to dedicate this book to our son Jimmy.
He's been our guinea pig for many of the projects
and has inspired us through his love of music and creativity.

Contents

Acknowledgments

Thank you to Bare Conductive for providing us with the Bare Conductive Touch Board Starter Kit and photos for use in this book.

Thank you to Inventables for permission to share a few projects here and allowing us to spread the love for Easel and the Carvey.

Thank you to the young makers who have participated in our music maker programs at the Middletown Free Library. Your participation in our programs was an inspiration in creating this work.

CHAPTER 1
Common Tools for Sound Creation

As with all maker projects, there are special tools, programs, and items you will need to get started with the audio projects presented in this book. You will need to figure out your budget and what kinds of projects you are interested in before diving into purchasing a lot of equipment.

The chapter will take a look at the wide variety of items available for creating sound projects. We will try to present several options for projects using tools and software that give you the most for your money and explore apps and software that are free or low in cost. For example, some audio recording software companies offer their products at several price points, and the number of features available is tied into the tier of software you purchase.

Many apps have a free "lite" version as well as a paid full version available. Sometimes it's a good idea to start off with the free or low-cost option and then move to the more expensive but feature-rich version once you become more familiar and are certain the app is something you wish to explore further and in more depth. Sometimes the free version will be all you need for your projects.

We will start off by taking a look at software and apps that can be used to create music and other types of audio projects. For those of you who are looking to dive into music making, this is the place to start. Here you will find the tools you can use to create your own music and sound creations. There are so many options out there that it can be difficult to identify the best software or app for your needs.

In this chapter, we hope to take some of that guess work out of the equation. We have identified the software and apps that are powerful but easy enough for beginner music makers to get started with. We have used these tools in makerspace programs at the Middletown Free Library and have explored them with our own young maker at home.

Some tools are not specialized pieces of equipment or software but very basic, cheap, and even *free* items that you probably already have on hand. For many of our programs with young and new music creators, we start out very simply using our bodies, drumsticks and buckets, or other everyday items to begin the learning process. Getting familiar with specialized terms, patterns, and other processes that go into music and sound creation becomes easier when learners can get acquainted with them in a physical way. By creating several entry points into the learning process, you can also address various learning styles, getting everyone not only to the point where they can start creating but also understanding the science behind some of the tools they will be using.

Music-Making Basics

Some of the best projects to get started with exploring music making and sound are simple tools and items that you can find around your house.

Drumsticks

Drumsticks are a great tool for more than just playing a drum. Grab a pair of drumsticks and a bucket, and you have created your own drum. You can also use the sticks to bang on something like a metal folding chair to explore low, middle, and high sounds.

Microphones

While our phones, tablets, and even many laptops are able to record audio, you may wish to invest in a microphone for better-quality sound recording. When you start looking into microphones, you will learn that there are several different types from which to choose. For the projects in this book, you are probably better served by choosing one microphone that can handle several different kinds of recording duties rather than purchasing specialty microphones. There are four general types of studio microphones available on the market today: condenser, dynamic, ribbon, and USB. The microphone you choose will depend on several factors, including your budget, what you want to use the microphone for, and the type of setup you have for recording audio.

Dynamic Microphone
A dynamic microphone is a good choice if you are interested in getting good audio but don't need the added sensitivity of a condenser mic. These mics are sturdy and

a good choice for recording when you don't have a soundproof room because they don't pick up as much background noise as a condenser mic. This is also a good choice for found sound projects, where you are trying to record a particular sound out in the field without picking up everything else that is going on around you.

Condenser Microphone

A condenser microphone is an excellent choice for recording spoken words or vocals. This kind of mic has a greater frequency and transient response that is able to reproduce the speed of the voice or instrument being recorded. Because of the way a condenser mic works, they are more fragile than a dynamic mic, so you may not want to use this kind of mic if you are going to be taking it out in the field to record. Condenser mics are also sensitive to loud sounds, so they are a much better choice when recording in a studio or quiet home location than in a place with a lot of background noise. Lastly, condenser mics need to be powered, so they are much less portable than dynamic mics. If your main goal is to record audio at home for a podcast, vocals for a song, or audio for a video, this is probably a great choice.

Ribbon Microphone

Ribbon microphones used to be very popular. A ribbon microphone is a very simple electrical design because it has no active circuitry. It is a bidirectional microphone that was most widely used from the 1930s through the 1950s. Ribbon microphones are starting to make a bit of a comeback, so you may come across one in your search. Also, because of their basic design, you can find do-it-yourself (DIY) kits to make your own ribbon microphone.

USB Microphone

A USB microphone is a good budget-conscious choice for those who are looking to get started recording sound without having to deal with a complicated interface or needing to have a mixer or other equipment. The Blue Snowball is a great choice for kids, beginners, or anyone looking to just plug and play or, in this case, record.

If your main workstation for audio recording is an iPad, you will need to purchase a USB-to-lightning camera adapter. This will allow you to use a USB microphone through the lightning port on your iPad.

Recycled and Found Objects and Craft Supplies

To learn the basics of the science behind sound and for just a fun and easy way to get started making music and sound, all you really need to do is look around your house, your classroom, and your neighborhood. You can invent your own instruments, making simple drums, tambourines, shakers, and more with just objects you probably already have lying around. There's no need to spend a lot of money on expensive instruments to start creating.

Digital Audio Workstation

A digital audio workstation (DAW) is the home base for those of you looking to record and delve into music-creation projects. Nowadays, your DAW can be a desktop computer or laptop as well as an iPad. Many of the popular sound recording and editing software programs are also available as apps, and for a hobbyist, an app can be a great and economical choice.

Recording and Editing Software and Apps

Audacity

If you are looking for an easy-to-use open-source software program that you can use to record and edit audio, Audacity is a good choice. This is a free, donation-supported audio editing and recording software for Windows, MAC, and Linux operating systems. If you are on a budget or just getting started with audio, a program such as Audacity is a great place to get started.

GarageBand

If you are a Mac user, GarageBand is already installed on your computer and you can get started recording, editing, and mixing your sound projects. The software provides virtual instruments, including Drummer, a virtual drum session player. You can even learn to play. If you switch between using your iPad and your Mac, the continuity of the interface is another nice feature of GarageBand. It's easy to use and get started with, so it's a natural choice for Mac users.

Cubase

Cubase is the software we use in our studio. It is made by a company called Steinberg, and there are three options you can choose from when selecting the software, depending on your needs and how much money you are looking to spend. We recommend for the beginner or hobbyist to go with Cubase Elements because it will give you everything you need to get started at around $100. Cubase Elements allows you to record and mix up to 48 audio tracks as well as 24 instrument tracks. The software also includes a mix console, sampler track, virtual instruments, and basic audio editing tools as well as other features. The Artist and Pro versions offer more features but come at a higher price. If you are using an iPad, there is Cubase iC Pro, a control app that has a focus on recording sound.

Ableton

Another popular choice, and one that you will often see mentioned in maker outlets for music projects, is Ableton. Like Cubase, it has three versions available that vary in price and features. For beginners, Ableton Live is a great place to start, and like Cubase Elements, it costs around $100 to purchase. This product allows you to record audio from any MIDI source, you can sample sounds, and a number of virtual instruments are available. Ableton Live also is a great choice for taking out of the studio and using for a performance because it's designed to use in a performance setting. Ableton has some great tutorials available on everything from learning the software to a great interactive walkthrough on making music in general that is worth checking out (https://learningmusic.ableton.com/).

While there are other software programs available, these are the ones that we feel are worth checking out for budget-minded beginners.

Apps for iPads

The iPad is the best tablet for music projects. A wealth of apps is available, and they are found only in the App Store. While some music-making apps are available for Android and Windows tablets, you won't find the wide selection of quality apps from industry leaders for these platforms. It should be noted that the Microsoft Surface Pro series of tablets allows software to be loaded on them so that you can create on the road. The projects presented in this book will focus on apps that are available on the iPad.

GarageBand

This is the app version of Apple's popular recording, editing, and mixing software. You can easily record and edit podcasts, create songs, and more with this easy-to-use and inexpensive app.

Korg iElectribe

The iElectribe is one of our favorite apps to use in music programs at the library's makerspace. This is a virtual analog beat box that is perfect for creating beats for your own musical creations. This is a great app that faithfully recreates the physical version of the software. You can also export your beats and easily upload your creations to SoundCloud. If you're a Gorillaz fan, even a Gorillaz version of the app is available that includes sounds created by the Gorillaz as well as preprogrammed patterns created by the band along with Korg. While you may balk at the $19.99 price tag, this app is often on sale for 50 percent off, so you can always wait for a sale to pick this up.

Korg Gadget

The Korg Gadget is a pretty unique app that will let you combine small synthesizers and drum machines, which Korg calls *Gadgets*, to create music in any number of genres. The app is $39.99 in the Apple App store, but note that a free "lite" version of the app is available as well. The free version does not give you access to as much functionality or the number of Gadgets that the free version does, but it's a great way to get started with Gadgets. If you are working on a Mac rather than an iPad, an even more powerful version of this tool is available that includes a plug-in collection. While it's great to have the added features that a desktop version offers, the iPad app offers access to a rich collection of creation tools and functionality.

Keezy and Keezy Drums

Keezy is a great app for people of all ages from toddlers to teens to seniors. Keezy is a very basic and easy-to-use sampler. You can use this app to create your own sound boards by recording a different sound onto each of the eight colored tiles. It comes preprogrammed with a variety of sound boards, including ones created by Reggie Watts.

If the iEclectribe is a bit too much for you, you can still create your own drum beats using Keezy Drummer. This is a simple drum machine that works similar to Keezy.

Jammer

Jammer is a free music-making app created by the Keezy Corporation. This app turns songs into pieces that you can use to create your own remix of sorts. You can choose any song that's available in the store for 30 seconds, but after that, you must purchase it for $0.99. This is a fun app to play around with but not a good choice for creating your own music.

Conductive Materials for Sound and Music Projects

Among the fun tools that can be found in many makerspaces are various ways for lighting up projects using conductive ink, copper tape, and e-textiles projects. Why not expand these tools to include sound and music projects? You can use these tools to create and expand projects with which you may already be familiar. Let's look at some of the conductive materials for adding sound and music elements to your projects. Some of these tools even allow you to create projects combining DAW software with the physical conductive project you create in the real world.

Bare Conductive Touch Board

Bare Conductive's conductive paint was one of the first tools I used in the maker programs at the Middletown Free Library. The paint works like any water-based paint and can be painted on surfaces to create interactive art projects. While you can use Bare Conductive's paint in simple paper electronics projects, the company also offers a power tool in the Touch Board that will allow you to really explore projects that combine conductive materials and music or sound. The Touch Board gives you endless possibilities for creating projects and includes an MP3 player as well as MIDI functionality. You can get started right out of the box without having to do any programming. Additionally, you can program it with an Arduino as well as touch and distance sensing. As you can tell, this is a pretty nifty tool that can be used with Bare Conductive's paint or other conductive material to create sound and music projects.

LilyPad

e-Textiles projects are a lot of fun and are another great way to bring sound and music to life in nontraditional ways. The LilyPad Arduino is relatively easy to get started with and is a programmable Arduino microprocessor used in sewing projects. Imagine the fun in creating your own plush creatures that make sound that you created when you press its hand or belly.

If programming is intimidating to you, you can still create fun wearable sound projects with the LilyPad MP3 player. You can load MP3 files onto this version of the LilyPad without having to program in the sounds. If you wish to tackle programming, you can also use the Arduino software to create your own sketches to load on the player. Soft circuits are a great activity that can combine many skills in one project. You can learn how to sew, design circuits and sound, and program in Arduino all in one project.

Makey Makey

The Makey Makey has become a staple in many makerspaces, especially in schools and libraries. This inexpensive "invention kit" acts as the mouse and keyboard when you hook it up to any material that can conduct electricity. You can hook it up to everyday objects such as fruit, aluminum foil, and other things to create all kinds of inventions. You can use the Makey Makey with software such as Ableton as well as the popular coding program Scratch to create your own projects combing real-world objects with software and coding elements.

micro:bit

The micro:bit is a small, fun, and easy-to-learn programmable computer that was designed to be used in educational settings to teach kids to code. You can learn to code JavaScript and Python with any web browser. There are apps for iOS and Android that allow you to use your phone or tablet to program the micro:bit as well. This is a great way to combine music projects with coding.

littleBits and the littleBits Korg Synth Kits

This is one our favorite tools to use with people of all ages to get started making music and learning the basics of circuits and the science behind sound. littleBits was founded by Ayah Bdeir in 2011 as a simple way for designers, artists, and engineers to get started prototyping projects without having to know how to solder, program, and so on. littleBits is great not only because all its kits work together but also because the company continues to introduce new bits of its own design and through partnerships with other organizations and creators.

The Korg Synth Kit is one of those products to grow out of such a partnership. This kit lets you build an analog modular synthesizer and is a great entry point for makers who would like to explore soft synths. The hands-on nature of the kit is great for tactile learners and easily allows you to break down and learn how each piece of the synthesizer works. Plus, there is the added satisfaction that comes from turning the knobs and adding in lights, triggers, and bits from the other littleBits kits.

littleBits has even introduced a Pro Kit to add to the Synth Kit that is great for those who really want to explore the power of the kit in music-creation projects. The MIDI bit, which allows you to send and receive MIDI messages, uses bits to create your own MIDI controller and even uses the Synth Kit with popular music software. The CV module allows you to connect your Synth Kit to other analog synthesizers. Lastly, the USB input-output (I/O) module allows you to record your Synth Kit compositions directly into your DAW. You can also use the USB I/O module to send signals to your Synth Kit.

As you can see, there are a lot of different and fun tools that you can explore as you hone your skills as a music and sound creator. We will be exploring these tools in the projects throughout this book.

CHAPTER 2
Music and Making

When one thinks of making and the maker movement, what often comes to mind are such things as 3D printers, robotics, and projects that light up, but one often does not think of a music-creation project as part of what is called *making*. However, if we think of the definition of *making*, the process of creating something, then we can see that music projects fit nicely into the maker movement and makerspaces.

While many people tend to think of making and makerspaces as activities and spaces where people engage with technology such as 3D printers, laser cutters, robotics, and the like, this is not a complete picture of what making is all about. When you visit a Maker Faire, you will see these kinds of activities, but you will also see artisans and crafters, people of all ages, making things out of everyday items and so much more. Projects that involve creating a piece of music, a dance performance, or even incorporating sound into more "traditional" maker projects are all under the maker tent.

Picture this scene: a room full of tweens ranging in age from about 11 to 14 years. They are sitting around the room, some on the floor, others at tables, engaged in conversation and working on iPads. They are bouncing around ideas and creating beats using the iElectribe app or maybe putting together the parts of a song they are creating on GarageBand. Most of them have little or no background in music creation, and some of them are not even that interested in music at this point in their lives, but they are working together to create something out of nothing. This is exactly what making is about!

Music is a powerful tool and is a great hook to get people involved in making whose interests may not lean toward coding, robotics, or 3D printed projects. Many people relate music and music creation to the arts, but it is also closely related to coding, and there are some who argue that musicians make great coders.

It is also important to meet makers where they are at and where their interests lie. Through the projects presented in this book, young music makers will have the opportunity to explore music and sound through a variety of projects that can help them figure out their interests and passions via something in which they are already interested. Budding filmmakers can learn about the process of recording and editing sound. The most important aspect of maker projects of any kind is using projects and new tools to create creators and doers, not just consumers.

Music and Sound Projects and Literacy

When one thinks of literacy, usually what springs to mind is activities around learning to read and write. In today's world, the idea of literacy is quickly expanding to encompass other kinds of learning as well. Much of this buzz centers around coding and the necessity for today's youth to learn how to code. But literacy in today's world is about more than just knowing how to read, write, and even code. Today's youth need to know how to communicate in the world they will be growing into, which means they need to be literate in more than just the traditional literacies. The idea of what it means to be literate is changing as fast as technology is changing.

The projects presented in this book are a great way to hone those twenty-first-century skills that is not always possible in traditional classrooms. Whether you are a librarian, parent, homeschooler, or just an interested adult, these skills are necessary to build for success in today's world. No matter what framework you look at, these four areas are agreed on as critical for future-ready students:

- Collaboration and teamwork
- Creativity, imagination, and out-of-the-box thinking
- Critical thinking
- Problem solving

Facts and information about a variety of topics are easier to access than at any time in history. Information is at our fingertips, but if a person is unable to think, collaborate, be creative, and solve problems, the access to this information is meaningless. Just as with any other skill, we are not born knowing how to do these things, but they can be taught and learned. Through high-interest projects, we can offer a fun and engaging way for students to learn and improve on these skills, making them ready to solve real-world problems.

Music and sound-creation programs can build on these skills while also incorporating other twenty-first-century skills that are critical to future success. For the purpose of this book, we'll look at twenty-first-century skills in an informal educational setting, as outlined by the Institute of Museum and Library Services (IMLS). There are broad areas of interest that are further broken down into more specific skill sets. Not all of these skills tie into the projects we will be exploring in this book, but with a little creativity and expansion on some of the projects, you can tie in areas we won't be spending as much time on. According to IMLS, these are the four broad skill areas that make up the twenty-first-century skill set:

- *Learning and innovation skills* include not only basic literacy but also such things as critical thinking and problem solving, creativity and innovation, communication and collaboration, and visual literacy and scientific and numerical thinking as cross-disciplinary thinking.
- *Information, media, and technology skills* cover such things as information and media literacy as well as being able to apply technology effectively.
- *Twenty-first-century themes* is a bit of a catch-all category that brings in global awareness as well as business, financial, and entrepreneurial skills, civic, health, and environmental literacy.
- *Life and career skills* include such things as flexibility and adaptability, initiative and self-direction, teamwork, leadership and responsibility, and productivity.

Whether you are an individual, homeschooler, librarian, or teacher, these skills are essential to success in the twenty-first century, and the projects in this book are a great place to start honing those skills while having fun.

Learning and Innovation Skills

Through sound and music projects, whether you are working with a digital or physical tool, learning and innovation skills are a vital part of creating a final product. When you are working in an app such as the iElectribe or working with the littleBits Synth, you will need to analyze and understand how the different parts of the app or tool work together to create the final output. Basic literacy is important whether you are writing a script for a podcast or lyrics for a song. Scientific and numerical literacy even come into play when you learn how a speaker works or are counting out beats to a song.

Information, Media, and Technology Skills

These skills seem like an obvious fit for sound and music-creation projects. Understanding copyrights when it comes to sampling or using sound bites in something like a podcast is a media literacy skill that is highly important when creating a project that will be shared on a place such as YouTube or SoundCloud. This skill area also includes such skills as analyzing and creating media. Interpreting song lyrics and music videos for message or even creating your own songs and accompanying videos would be a great way to hone media literacy through music.

Twenty-First-Century Themes

While this skill may not appear to be an obvious fit for sound and music-creation projects, there are connections that you can make to real-life applications based on the projects in this book. Songs, podcasts, or videos could be created incorporating topics of health, the environment, or civics. You can explore instruments and music from other cultures, comparing them with your own culture's popular music. As part of the podcasting project, you can explore financial, business, and entrepreneurial literacy through the business models of podcasts, advertising, and figuring out how a podcast can become profitable.

Life and Career Skills

Through the projects presented in this book, you will be exploring a variety of topics that can help you to identify things that interest you and use them as a springboard to learning about careers. Because the projects presented in this book can be used in a group setting or individually, there are opportunities to work on skills such as self-directed learning, working independently, and working in a team or setting goals for learning.

Sample Project

A multiweek program can be a great way to incorporate these twenty-first-century skills into your music and sound-creation projects. Whether you are a homeschooler, teacher, parent, or librarian, you can get participants creating while working on developing these skills. Through the Music-Creation Club program, students will work with all the larger twenty-first-century skills.

Learning and innovation skills are a part of every week of the program. Students will learn to think and work creatively with their fellow club members. By writing lyrics, students will be working with basic literacy skills that also fall under this category. Lastly, students will work on their collaboration and communication skills. When listening to favorite songs, they will work on listening for meaning and think about whether the song is an effective way to communicate a message. In the lyric-writing session, students will collaborate to come up with a song idea and some lyrics to help them think about the final song they will be creating.

Information, media, and technology skills are obviously a big part of the program. Club members will be working with a variety of digital tools to create their final projects. They will learn how to share their creations with a wider audience by uploading their work to SoundCloud. You could even expand the club to include the creation of music videos and add a segment where students watch and interpret music videos. Being able to decode media messages and create their own media to communicate ideas are both part of this skill area.

Twenty-first-century themes are really only loosely connected to a music-creation club as outlined here. However, you could definitely tie in these themes with club activity. During week three, when club members will listen to songs and deconstruct them, you could add in some examples of music from other countries, adding a global perspective to the club. You could also challenge your club members to create songs that have a message involving environmental, civic, or health themes.

Lastly, life and career skills are easy to incorporate into club activities. Students will learn about flexibility as they work on their songs, incorporating suggestions and ideas from fellow club members and club leaders. Having a goal of a showcase of their work at the last session will help them to work with deadlines and learn how to manage their time in order to complete the project. They will even need to be responsible to their partners and interact in an effective manner with that person to make sure that everyone's ideas are incorporated into the work. Some students may choose to work on their own for the final project, which again ties in because these students will be working on their independent and self-directed learning skills.

Music-Creation Club Program Outline

Week One

In the first week, we'll get started with learning the skills needed to lay the foundation of a song, the beat. In this sessions, participants will work through the drum sequencing activity in Chapter 4. They will get acquainted with the iElectribe app and lay down their first beats. Participants can work in pairs or individually for this project. Let the students spread out so that they can collaborate and work on their projects without disturbing other students at their table. At our club meetings, kids sat on pillows on the floor around the room and at tables as they worked through their projects.

Week Two

In this session, we'll get started with the littleBits Synth Kit as your club works through the lesson in Chapter 4. This session helps to lay the foundation for learning how a synthesizer works, as well as acquainting students with the terminology they will encounter when they move into learning to use recording and editing software such as GarageBand or Ableton. Ask participants to have a favorite song ready to share with the group at the next session.

Week Three

This session will be spent listening to everyone's favorite song. We'll analyze each song for such things as song structure, instrumentation, and lyrical content. You will probably be surprised at the mix of genres that will be represented by the picks. When we ran this session at the Middletown Free Library, the tweens' song picks included songs from the '50s and '60s, current pop hits, emo classics, and electronic dance music (EDM). It was a great mix of tunes and provided for an interesting analysis. You may wish to have some songs ready to supplement the participants' picks if there is not much variety or to add a global view to the program.

Week Four

This week the participants will dive into learning how to record a song using GarageBand using the knowledge they have gained from the first three sessions. They will learn how to use the instruments available in the app to create a song base. They will also learn how to record vocal tracks using a microphone and iPad.

Week Five

At this session, participants will learn about the final piece of the music-creation puzzle that will be covered in this program, lyric writing. Start out the session by thinking about the songs the students shared during week three's session. Have the students discuss what the songs were about, and if they are having a hard time remembering, you can always relisten to a few of the selections. You can also have the students brainstorm ideas for what kinds of things songs are about in general, such as love, sadness, politics, and so on.

Once you have talked about the lyrics of other people's songs, have the group start thinking about what they would like to write about. For this session, it may be best to brainstorm the ideas for lyrics as a group depending on the age of the group with which you are working. Elementary and middle school kids often have a harder time coming up with ideas to write about. If students are working individually or in smaller groups, give them the time to work and be available if they have questions or need help.

Weeks Six and Seven

These two weeks will be the work sessions where students will work to create their own musical creations using the skills and tools they have honed in previous sessions. Make the littleBits Synth Kits, iElectribe, and GarageBand apps available and any other tools you used in previous weeks so that students can explore how they want to create their own songs. It is also important to provide paper and pencils as well as a quiet space for each creator to work. If you only have a single room available, allow students to sit on the floor and move around to find a place to work and listen. You may wish to provide headphones as well. It is important for you as the instructor to move around and check in with the groups to be sure that they are making progress and to address any questions students may have. You also may want to emphasize that while students are working toward a showcase of their tunes, they don't have to present a completed work.

Week Eight

This is the day when students will have the opportunity to showcase what they have been working on. For our final session, we provided about 30 minutes at the beginning for students to put the finishing touches on their work and get help with any aspects with which they are having trouble. We then invited families in for a showcase of everyone's work. Each team or individual had a chance to get up and play his or her song for the assembly. Each team or individual gave a short introduction, played the song, and then our instructors asked some questions about the song. Showcasing is so important when running any kind of maker programs. Most people love to show off what they have created, and when you are working with young people, their families really enjoy seeing the results of what their children have been learning. As part of this session, you can also teach your club members how to upload their creations to SoundCloud. You could have each student create his or her own account or use an account created for your club. You can listen to some of our club members' creations on SoundCloud at https://soundcloud.com/user-32020755.

Music and Sound Projects and Making

As technology has become just a part of everyday life, interest in learning how that technology works is waning. Many people just want their technology to work. but they are not particularly interested in why or how it works. Through immersive, hands-on learning experiences that combine the digital and real worlds, that spark to find out "why" can be struck.

In *Free to Make: How the Maker Movement Is Changing Our Schools, Our Jobs, and Our Minds,* (2016) Dale Dougherty tells us, "The process of realizing an idea and making it tangible is what defines a maker." Makers are creative, and they take their ideas and bring them to life either through skills they already have or by picking up new skills while creating something. What is created may be a digital creation, a physical creation, or a combination of both. Makers are creators.

The maker movement can be seen to have gained some of its inspiration from the do-it-yourself (DIY) mind-set that has always been a big part of the punk rock movement from its beginnings in the 1970s to today. Punk rock flea markets feature a variety of artists selling handmade items ranging from t-shirts to furniture to clocks. If you have the opportunity to visit one of the many Maker Faires held around the world, you will see the natural fit music has with the world of making. You will see homemade instruments, kits to build your own Theremin or Bluetooth speaker, and people performing their own EDM compositions.

The rise of technology as an essential part of everyday life has led to a glut of devices, apps, and choices available to students and makers. This can be seen in the number of music apps and other available technology that can make anyone with an iPad or computer into a musician or producer. While technology has made access to tools that were once reserved for professionals very easy, many people are getting into creating without diving deeply into the tools they are using, instead being satisfied with preprogrammed sounds and beats rather than learning how to use them as starting points to creating their own sounds. Many of us listen to music everyday but never think about what goes on behind the scenes to make a song come to life or even think about how the technology we use to listen to a song works. Exploring these ideas and figuring how something works by taking it apart or breaking it down into its most basic form are tasks that are integral to makers and making. If you understand how something works, whether it's an instrument, a piece of software, or an app, you will be able to solve any number of problems you encounter along the way because you have an intimate knowledge of how it works.

As you can see, music and sound creation can be an integral part to any makerspace. You can combine the physical and digital to create something new or as a hands-on approach to learning that can go back and forth between both worlds. Tools such as the Bare Conductive Touch Board or the LilyPad MP3 player even provide the means to combining both worlds. Makers are creators, they are curious, and they are doers. The projects presented in this book will put you on a path from music listener to music creator and maker.

Music, Youth, and Identity

Music can be a powerful force in people's lives. As one enters the middle school years, music not only becomes an increasingly important part of one's life but often is also instrumental in shaping one's identity. Songs tell stories and open doors to new worlds for listeners in much the same way that books do. We take a journey as we listen to a song and sometimes an entire album as the story unfolds with each song. Our favorite artist is there for us when we're feeling down and when we're celebrating, exercising, or even just relaxing. With the advent of the Internet and streaming services, the world of music is available to us at the touch of a finger on a screen.

Much of the way in which music helps one find one's identity is through the artists who create the music with which the listener identifies. Perhaps the listener adopts the style of dress or politics of their favorite artists or musical genre. But what if the listener was given the tools and had the door opened to start creating his or her own music and creating his or her own identity through their own creations rather than just by consuming the creations of others? Obviously, there have always been people who take up instruments and start a band, but for many this seems out of reach or just something of dreams. However, when you provide opportunities through maker activities focused on music and sound creation, you are opening the door to a possibility that the participant may have never realized is out there.

By narrowing down the hundreds of apps and tools that are out there for music and sound creation, you make it easier for a budding maker to start creating rather than trying to find the app that is just right to get started. Through the projects in this book, we'll help open this door.

CHAPTER 3
Exploring Sound

A great place to get started with music and sound projects is to go back to the basics using simple materials that you may have lying around the house or that are easily obtainable and inexpensive. You can use these homemade instruments to explore how sound is made.

Sound is made when something causes the air to vibrate. These vibrations travel through the air in waves, called *sound waves*. We hear the sound because these sound waves reach our ears and cause our ear drums to vibrate. This vibration sends a signal to our brain that carries the information telling our brain what sound it is hearing. Sound waves can travel through materials such as liquids and solids as well. The material the sound travels through affects how it sounds.

Found Sound Band

Below is a list of materials that you will need to make various instruments to explore the science of how we hear sound, including vibration and pitch. Get your friends together and create your own found sound band to create some unique music pieces!

Materials

- Empty coffee cans and other containers of various sizes and materials
- Empty cardboard boxes, toilet paper rolls, paper towel rolls
- Balloons
- Window shrink film, cellophane wrap, or other plastic wrap
- Rubber bands of various thicknesses

- Hairdryer
- Drumsticks
- Pencils
- Straws
- Paper and plastic cups
- Jars or glasses
- Double-sided tape, masking tape, and/or duct tape
- Any other materials you think would be good for creating an instrument

Make Your Own Drums

There are several ways you can make your own drums. The sound you hear a drum make depends on the material the drum is made out of as well as the size, shape, and tension of the drum head. Some drums are played with your hands, whereas others are played with a stick or brush depending on the type of drum and/or the sound you are looking for. For this project, we'll experiment with sound by making drums out of different sized containers and with different materials for the drum head.

Drum One

For this drum, we'll need an empty coffee can, a balloon, and some rubber bands. The first thing you will want to do is observe the material the can is made out of. Some coffee cans are made out of metal and others out of a heavy lined cardboard or even plastic. Try finding a few coffee cans made of different materials to see if you get different sounds. Once you have your coffee can cleaned and dried, you are ready to make the drum head.

Step One
Cut the neck off one of your balloons, and then stretch the balloon over the open top of the coffee can. To make your drum sturdier, repeat with a second balloon (Figure 3.1).

Step Two
Secure the double layer of balloons to the can with a rubber band or two. If you don't have rubber bands, you can secure the balloons in place with masking tape (Figure 3.2).

Figure 3.1   Fit one balloon over top of can, then repeat with the second balloon.

Figure 3.2   Place a rubber band over the can to hold balloons in place.

HINT: Be sure to get big enough balloons so that they don't break easily when you stretch them to fit over the can.

Drum Two

For this drum, you will need a number of containers of various sizes, window shrink film, double-sided tape, masking tape, and a hairdryer.

Step One

Place your container on a flat surface, and cut a piece of the window shrink film to fit over the top of the container with enough overage to hang about halfway down the side of the container. If you don't have window shrink film, you can try plastic wrap or cellophane for your drum head (Figure 3.3).

FIGURE 3.3   Hold a sheet of the plastic over your bowl to figure out how much you will need to fit over your container.

Step Two

Place double-sided tape around the sides of your container about 2 inches from the top (Figure 3.4).

Figure 3.4   Place the double-sided tape around the bowl about 2 inches from the top.

Step Three

Place the shrink film over the top of the container, and push the overhanging sides of the shrink wrap onto the double-sided tape (Figure 3.5).

Figure 3.5   Place your plastic over the bowl and press down on the tape to hold in place.

Step Four

Place masking tape around the plastic wrap near the top on the sides of the container (Figure 3.6).

Figure 3.6   Use masking tape around the top of the bowl to make an even tighter fit.

Step Five

Use your hairdryer on the hot setting to "shrink" the plastic to get a nice tight fit (Figure 3.7).

Step Six

Test your drum using your drumsticks or other item you have around that can be used like a drumstick (Figure 3.8).

Try making drums out of containers of different sizes and materials. How does the size change the sound you hear? Does the material out of which you make your drum affect the way it sounds? Do the drums made with a balloon drum head sound different from the ones made with plastic wrap drum heads?

Figure 3.7   Use a hairdryer to shrink the plastic in place and make a tight drum head.

Figure 3.8   Use a set of drumsticks, pencils, etc., to test out your drum.

You can observe the vibration of sound by using the drums you just made. First, observe the drum by hitting it with a drumstick to see if you notice any vibration. You will probably not notice the drum head vibrating when you just hit it with a stick, even though we know that this is what's happening. Next, place a small amount of rice, beads, or other small objects on the drum head; this works really well with the drum you made using the balloons. Next, strike the drum head hard enough so that you can hear a sound but not so hard that your materials go flying off the top of the drum. You should see the objects moving after you strike the drum. This is the vibration of the sound you hear. You can also feel this vibration by placing a few fingers lightly on your throat and then making a humming sound. You will feel the vibration as the sound you are making.

You can also use the GarageBand app to see this vibration in action. Open the app on your iPad, and select BASS or GUITARS. Use one of the stringed bass guitars available and hold down on one of the strings, making sure that AUTOPLAY is in the OFF position. You will see the string vibrating very fast at first; then it slows down and stops as the sound gets softer. If you have the switch set on CHORDS, you will see the entire string vibrate. If it's set on NOTES, you'll only see the portion of the string to the right of your finger vibrate (Figure 3.9).

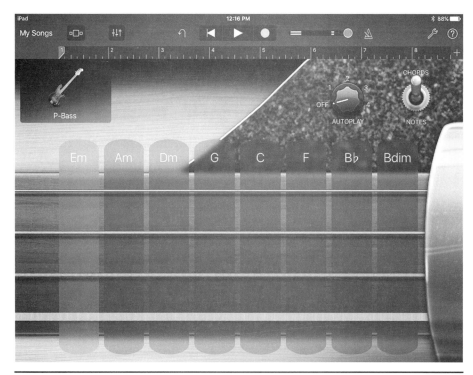

Figure 3.9 You can see the vibration causing sound by plucking a bass string in GarageBand.

Exploring Pitch and Sound Waves in Your Found Sound Band

Make Your Own Guitar or Stringed Strumming Instrument

Materials

- Empty cardboard boxes (cereal boxes, tissue boxes, and flat packing boxes are great)
- Rubber bands of various widths
- Scissors
- Tape
- Paper towel rolls (optional)
- Craft supplies to decorate your stringed instrument

Step One

Choose your box, and cut a hole out of the center or wherever you would like the hole to be if you are making a guitar. If you have a packing box, tape the top closed if you want to cut a hole out for a guitar or cut off the flaps to have a large opening (Figures 3.10 and 3.11).

FIGURE 3.10 Cut a hole somewhere in the center of your box.

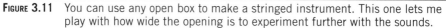

FIGURE 3.11   You can use any open box to make a stringed instrument. This one lets me play with how wide the opening is to experiment further with the sounds.

Step Two

Place some rubber bands around the box over the hole or the whole box if you are making an open-box instrument. You can place the rubber bands vertically or horizontally; it doesn't matter (Figures 3.12 and 3.13).

FIGURE 3.12 Cereal box bass.

FIGURE 3.13 Open box player.

Step Three

If you want to make your box look more like a guitar, you can tape the paper towel holder to the top of the box. Then you can decorate your box (Figure 3.14).

FIGURE 3.14   Found sound string section.

Now that you have your guitar completed, pluck on the strings to see how it sounds. Does the thickness of the rubber band affect the sound you hear? Think about the sounds of guitars you hear in music. A bass guitar has a thick, deep sound, whereas an acoustic or electric guitar makes higher-pitched sounds. The pitch is the frequency at which the sound waves vibrate. In general, a smaller object makes a higher-pitched sound and a larger object a lower-pitched sound. Thus you may notice in your guitar project that the thinner rubber bands make a higher sound than the thicker rubber bands. Going back to GarageBand, you can once again open the BASS or even better the GUITAR so that you can see this in a more visible way. The thinner strings at the top make a higher sound than the thicker strings at the bottom.

Now that you have some drums and a guitars, you are ready to rock out! You can also challenge yourself to see if you can create other instruments using everyday items you can find in your house, classroom, or around town. With your family, friends, or classmates, you could have a fun evening creating a song or two using these instruments. Performing for your friends, family, or classmates would be a great way to showcase your hard work, or you could record a video of your found sound band performance and share it on YouTube.

Exploring Loudness/Intensity and Amplitude with Speakers

Taking things apart is always a great way to see how things work. However, this is not always the most practical way to go, especially when we are talking about expensive items such as synthesizers, speakers, or other powered musical instruments. So, if you don't have a speaker you can take apart, you have several options for making your own speaker.

There are many kits available for purchase that will teach you how a speaker works by building your own. Some of these kits require soldering skills, so you need to keep that in mind when you look into this option.

- *Technology Will Save Us Speaker Kit.* This is a great kit for someone who is looking for a more involved soldering project. With this kit, you will be soldering all the components of the speaker to the circuit board. If you are looking to get deeper into electronics and building your soldering skills, this is a great kit.
- *BOSEbuild Speaker Cube.* This is a great choice if you are looking to learn more about sound and how a speaker works. No soldering is involved, and the speaker can be completely built in about 5 minutes. That's a great feature if you just want to listen to some music, but the real beauty of this kit is that it allows you to easily see each component that is used to make a speaker, and you can use a few parts to do experiments to learn about sound. In addition, there is a companion iOS app with a variety of lessons to use with the Speaker Cube to learn more. You can look at sound waves by experimenting with frequency or make a working speaker with just a coil of wire and magnet.

If you don't want to spend a lot of money on a kit, you can always make a basic speaker with everyday objects you already have or parts that are easily salvaged from nonworking electronics you probably have stashed away somewhere in your home.

Materials

- Paper or styrofoam bowl
- Paper plate
- Round magnets that can be stacked
- Copper magnet wire (this can be purchased inexpensively or you can salvage some from old electronics; be sure to do this carefully and with an adult)
- A sheet of paper
- Hot glue gun
- Scissors
- Soldering iron and solder (optional)
- Earbuds (optional)

Step One

Stack about five or six of the magnets on top of each other to form a cylinder (Figure 3.15).

FIGURE 3.15   Stack about five or six magnets on top of each other.

Step Two

Cut a strip of the paper, and wrap it around your tower of magnets. Then tape the paper to itself to keep it closed. Take another strip of paper, and wrap it around the tower of magnets that is now wrapped up in the first piece of paper. Tape it to itself to keep it closed. Do not tape the two pieces of paper to each other because you will need to remove the inner piece of paper later in the project (Figures 3.16 and 3.17).

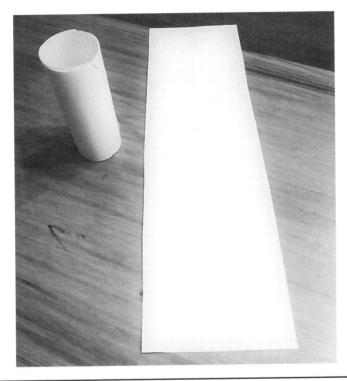

Figure 3.16   Wrap two strips of paper around the magnets, one at a time.

Figure 3.17   Both strips of paper are now wrapped around the magnets.

Step Three

Wrap your copper wire around the paper and magnet tower about 50 times. Use a small amount of hot glue to hold the wire in place. Wait for the hot glue to cool before moving on to the next step (Figure 3.18).

Step Four

Remove the inner tube of paper and magnets from your magnet and paper tower. You will now have one tube that consists of the magnets wrapped in one layer of paper and a second tube of paper with the copper wire attached to the outside. This tube of paper with the copper wire around it is called the *voice coil* (Figure 3.19).

Figure 3.18   Wrap the copper wire around the outer tube.

Figure 3.19   Remove the inner tube and magnets from the paper tube tower so you have two tubes.

Step Five

The voice coil is too long as is, so you will need to cut it down to a smaller size. It needs to be long enough to slip over the stack of magnets. Once it's the right size, hot glue the voice coil to the bottom of your paper plate (Figures 3.20 and 3.21).

FIGURE 3.20   Cut down the tube with the copper wire on it to just fit over the magnets.

FIGURE 3.21   Glue the tube with the copper wire to the bottom side of your paper plate.

Step Six

Next, you are going to take the bowl and cut some holes into the side; this will make it look more like a traditional speaker basket (Figure 3.22).

FIGURE 3.22 Cut holes in the sides of your bowl to resemble a speaker.

Step Seven

Hot glue the magnet stack, without the paper around it, to the bottom of the bowl. Place the voice coil over the magnet stack in the bowl and glue the plate to the bowl to keep it in place (Figures 3.23 and 3.24).

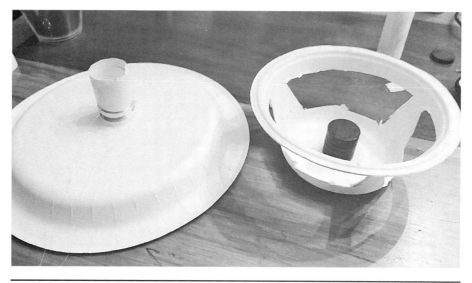

FIGURE 3.23   This is what your two pieces should look like at this point.

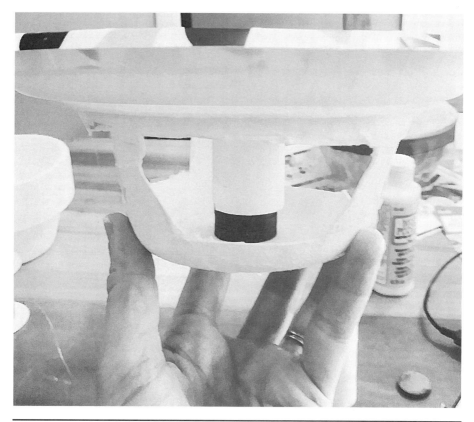

FIGURE 3.24   Glue the plate to the bowl to make the speaker house.

Step Eight

You now need to remove the insulation from the ends of the copper wire. You can do this with sandpaper, but be sure to be very gentle or you could accidentally remove some of the copper wire. You could also use a lighter or open flame from a match or candle with adult supervision to quickly remove this coating.

Step Nine A

One way to connect your speaker to a device to play sound is to use alligator clips to attach the two ends of copper wire to a stereo or television with a built-in amplifier. Turn on the device, and you should hear sound coming from your speaker.

Step Nine B

Another option for connecting your speaker to a device to play sound is to use an old pair of earbuds. To use old earbuds, cut the earbud wire where it splits into two pieces. Use wire strippers to remove the outer insulation, exposing the wires underneath. You should see four wires: two copper, one red, and one green. As a precaution, use the method in Step Eight to be sure that there is no remaining insulation on the copper wires; then twist them together. Next, strip about half of the outer insulation off the green and red wires, exposing the copper wire underneath. Twist these wires together. Solder the wires from the speaker coil to the headphone wire. Plug the speaker jack into your phone or other device, and play your favorite tune (Figures 3.25 through 3.27)!

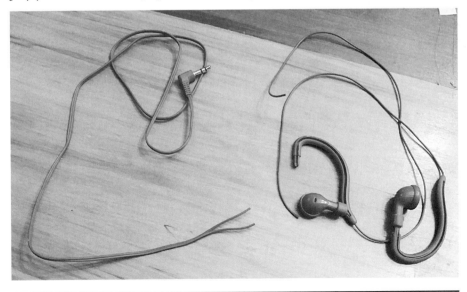

FIGURE **3.25**   Cut the headphones into two pieces.

Figure 3.26   The wires are small but you will see the red and copper color on the wires.

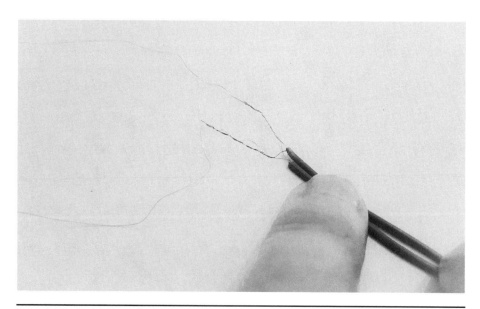

Figure 3.27   Twist the red wires together and then the copper wires together.

A speaker is a relatively simple object, and this easy homemade speaker is perfect for observing how speakers work. As you can see, a speaker is made up of three important components: a magnet, a coil of magnetic wire, and a cone. As we saw in our previous creations, sound is created when something causes air to vibrate, creating a sound wave. When audio is recorded using a microphone, the sound is stored as electrical signals. When you play audio, whether it's from your smartphone or on a turntable, the electrical signal is turned into an electric current. This current is then received by the speaker, which converts it back into sound waves. You can often observe the vibration of the diaphragm in many traditional speakers.

In the speaker we just built, there is a stack of magnets that are permanent magnets and copper wire wrapped around the piece of paper acting as our voice coil, which is an electromagnet. In a permanent magnet, there is always a north end and a south end, known as its *polar orientation*. In an electromagnet, the polar orientation is not set, and the magnet can rearrange its polarization.

Your audio source can also be called an *amplifier* because it is a device that increases the strength of an electric signal. The amplifier is always changing the direction in which the electric signal is traveling. The positively and negatively charged particles, called *current*, are constantly going through the speaker, moving one way and then reversing direction. This is called an *alternating current*, and this is what causes the polar orientation to keep reversing itself.

Because the alternating current changes direction as it flows through the voice coil, the polar orientation reverses, and the diaphragm will move back and forth because the magnetic force created between the voice coil and the permanent magnet is changing, which makes the voice coil move back and forth. As you can see in the speaker you made, the voice coil is attached to the speaker cone, and the back-and-forth movement of the coil causes the speaker cone to move back and forth, creating sound waves. The electric audio signal can also be interpreted as waves, and the frequency (pitch) and amplitude (change in the peaks) of those waves, which is perceived as loudness, determine how the voice coil moves, thus determining the sound waves that are produced from the diaphragm. This also affects how you hear the sound (Harris 2001).

Google *Science Journal* Activity

Materials
- Smartphone with Android OS
- Google *Science Journal* app

- Homemade instruments and speaker
- Other sources of sound

Now that we know how a speaker works, we can do some simple experimenting using the Google *Science Journal* app to measure the intensity of sound, which is measured in a unit called a *decibel*. The intensity of a sound is affected by the amplitude at which the sound wave is vibrated. The amount of distance a vibrating object moves when it vibrates is its *intensity*. This is perceived by us as loudness. A quieter sound will have a longer waveform with small peaks, whereas a louder sound will have shorter waveforms with high peaks.

The Google *Science Journal* app can be used to record the intensity of sounds in *decibels* (dB). The human ear is very sensitive, with the ability to hear something as quiet as 0 dB. Decibels are measured on a scale, but don't be tricked into thinking that a sound at 20 dB is twice as loud as a sound at 10 dB. The scale can be a little odd in that in this example the sound at 20 dB is 100 times louder than the 10-dB sound. When thinking about loudness and hearing, remember that a sound does not have to be painful to be harmful to your hearing. Anything above 85 dB can be harmful, so when you are playing sounds to measure their intensity, keep this in mind.

For this activity, we'll measure the intensity of the sounds made by the objects we just created. Feel free to throw in any other sounds that you would like to measure. Perhaps you want to measure the intensity of the sound coming from your headphones or your TV. Keep in mind that the intensity of the recorded sound depends on several factors, including:

- The distance between the phone and the source of the sound
- Where the source of the sound is located, that is, in front of you, behind you, above you, or below you
- Whether you are outside or inside
- Interference from other noise in your environment

Step One

Install the *Science Journal* app from the Play Store if you haven't already done so. This is a free app.

Step Two

Open the app, and click on the small arrow at the top of the screen where it says, "Untitled Experiment." Tap on New Experiment, and give your experiment a title and description (Figure 3.28).

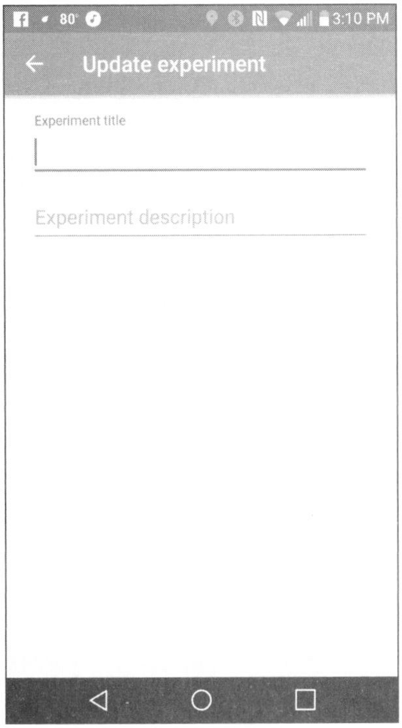

FIGURE **3.28**   Give your sound experiment a name.

Step Three

Tap the icon that looks like a speaker to open the intensity reader. You should see a small speaker with a reddish-pink half-circle flashing, representing the sound coming out of the speaker. In the room where I am writing this, I can hear the sound of my typing, outside road noise, and the quiet sounds of my officemate's music. The intensity reading is fluctuating between 24 and 34 dB.

Step Four

Decide what you wish to record, and press the red Record button at the bottom of the screen (Figure 3.29).

Figure 3.29   Tap the red record button to record the decibel levels of your sound.

Step Five

When you are done recording, press the red Record button again, and you'll see the report on the intensity of your sound (Figure 3.30).

You can make notes to record conditions at a certain point in time in your measurement or just note the conditions in which you made the recording. You may wish to record the same sound under different conditions, such as close to the source of the sound, further away from the source, or generally in a noisy or quiet environment. Name each recording you make if you wish to make comparisons with other sounds or conditions (Figure 3.31).

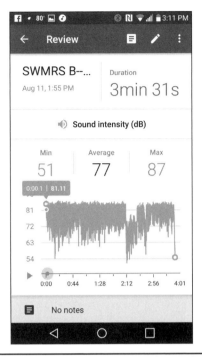

FIGURE 3.30   Once you are done recording you can see the results of your experiment.

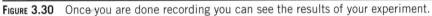

FIGURE 3.31   Name each recording to make it easy to compare readings.

You also may wish to compare your sound's intensity versus other sounds on the decibel scale. Here's a list of some common sounds and where they fall on the scale:

- 0 dB: healthy hearing threshold
- 30 dB: a whisper
- 60 dB: normal conversation
- 90 dB: lawn mower
- 110 dB: rock band
- 125 dB: balloon popping (Fox 2017)

Now that you have had fun using basic materials to learn about the science behind sound and music, you can get started digging deeper into more sophisticated tools used for creation.

References

Fox, Sarinne. 2017. "Noise Level Chart." *Noise Help*. Available at www.noisehelp.com/noise-level-chart.html (accessed August 11, 2017).

Harris, Tom. 2001. "How Speakers Work." HowStuffWorks.com (February 2, 2017). Available at http://electronics.howstuffworks.com/speaker.htm (accessed August 11, 2017).

CHAPTER 4
Making Sound

Making Sound with littleBits

littleBits is one of our favorite tools to use at the library's makerspace, CreateSpace@MFL. The kits are easy to get started with, and people of all ages love exploring and creating with the bits so much that we have begun circulating kits at the library. Our space is an official littleBits Global Chapter, so we create programming around the bits on a regular basis. littleBits is a great tool for making on the go. The bits are easy to pack up in the tackle box and take with you, and storage is a snap!

While we are lucky at CreateSpace to have Isaac as the leader of our littleBits music-making programs, the kit is so easy to use that just about anyone can lead a program or teach a class with it.

Materials

- *littleBits Synth Kit*. Kids can work in pairs or individually.
- *littleBits mounting boards*. While these are not required, they are a nice way to keep your project in place while you are working on it.
- *Extra bits*. You can use light sensors and light-emitting diodes (LEDs) to expand your creations and experiment with adding new elements to trigger sound.

Age Range and Class Size

We've run this program with kids as young as seven years old, but kids that young do better with the assistance of a parent or adult. The ideal age for kids to work independently would be ages nine and up. Because each Synth Kit comes with only enough bits to build one complete synthesizer, the group size is limited to the number of kits your library space owns. You can work individually, but it's more fun to pair up and work together. We recommend no more than two or three kids per kit in order to ensure that collaboration and learning are really happening.

Time Frame

This program runs about 90 minutes, giving the kids time to explore sound and share their creations.

Getting Familiar with the Synth Kit and littleBits

If you have never used littleBits before, you will want to familiarize yourself with the color-coding system that all littleBits kits use. Once you are familiar with this, you can combine kits to expand your projects and ideas because all kits use the same coding system.

- *Blue bits.* These are your power supply. Most kits come with a battery-operated power bit that runs off a 9-volt battery. The other option is the USB power bit, which you can connect to your computer or wall charger.
- *Pink bits.* These are your inputs, such as triggers, buttons, switches, and so on. You will notice that your Synth Kit is composed primarily of these pink input bits. The input tells the system what should happen with the output, whether it's shaping a sound, creating a tone, or sending a voltage. The inputs are the heart of the Synth Kit.
- *Green bits.* These are your outputs. Your Synth Kit comes with one very important output, the speaker. Other kits include outputs such as LEDs, buzzers, and vibrating motors just to name some of our young makers' favorite bits.
- *Orange bits.* These are your wires and other ways to branch out and extend your projects. You can expand your Synth Kit with the Pro Audio add-on, which includes three orange bits that are specific to music-making projects. The MIDI bit allows you to send and receive MIDI messages. The USB input-output (I/O) bit allows you to record audio directly to your computer or digital audio workstation. The Control Voltage (CV) bit allows you to use your Synth Kit with other analog synths that you may have. In this book, we will only concern ourselves with the USB I/O bit

because the other bits would include more advanced projects that are outside the scope of this work.

Project

Now that you have some background on littleBits and how they work, you are ready to dive into a project.

What You Do

This program consists of four parts; in the first part, you will be using your body to generate tones and learning how to mimic the various synth bits, and at the end, you will put all the pieces together to create tones with the bits.

Your body will serve as the power supply for this project. You will then use your mouth, voice, and hands to mimic various parts of the synthesizer. Here is a breakdown of how you can use your body to mimic the synth parts:

- *Oscillator*. Using your voice to generate a tone.
- *Envelope*. Using your mouth in the shape of an envelope to form sound.
- *Filter*. Hand over ears.

To prepare for the littleBits portion of the program, you will need to arrange the pieces of the Synth Kit into a chain consisting of a single oscillator, envelope, filter, and speaker. If you are teaching a group or using this project as part of a class, you will want to create a chain of littleBits to use as a demonstration. The bits should be arranged in the following order (Figure 4.1):

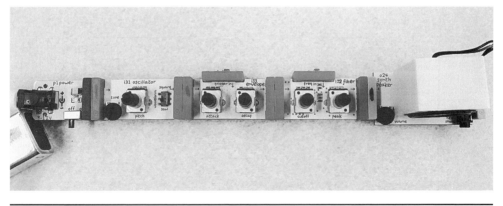

Figure 4.1   These are the bits we will work with for this project.

- *Power supply*. This bit gives you the ability to use a 9-V battery to supply power to the bits attached.
- *Keyboard*. This bit is a series of switches organized in a fashion similar to a piano keyboard, which enables you to trigger/play your creation as a melody. Note that this is a mono instrument, so only one note can be played at a time when arranging the bits in a more "traditional" manner.
- *Oscillator*. This bit is a tone generator that gives you control over the sound's tune and pitch via a dial and knob.
- *Envelope*. This bit shapes the sound in terms of loudness.
- *Filter*. This bit alters a sound's timbre by either exciting or diminishing certain frequencies.
- *Speaker*. This tiny yet mighty bit allows you to hear the sounds that you have created and includes an ⅛-inch headphone jack for more "private listening" and experimentation.

If you are teaching this project for a class, you may wish to start with this short introduction to the lesson: "Today we will become human synthesizers, and then we will get to build and play with a real synthesizer."

For this project, you will begin by using your own body as a power supply; your mind and body will power your noise making!

Step One

To start, think about a unique sound you can make with your mouth. Some examples include the "vroom" sound of a car and the "boo" sound of a ghost. This step works best if your noise has a long vowel sound. Take a few minutes to play around with sounds and practice making sounds.

If you are teaching a class, have the group sit in a circle, and go around the circle asking each participant to showcase the mouth sound he or she has chosen. You may want to have each participant name his or her sound to make discussion easier and as practice for creating sounds for projects.

Once everyone has shared his or her sound or you have played around with making a few sounds, take out the littleBits oscillator. Your voice is like an oscillator. The oscillator is the heart of your synthesizer and will be the main source of sound for your creations. This bit consists of a knob that allows you to adjust the pitch of your tone, a dial for tuning, and lastly a switch that allows you to change the shape of the sound.

Waveforms come in two shapes, square and saw-toothed. A square wave has a rich sound, whereas a saw-toothed wave sound can be described as a softer, round sound (Figure 4.2).

Waveforms

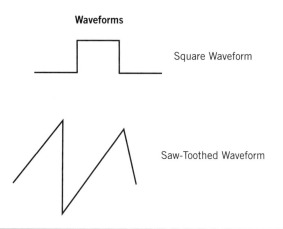

Square Waveform

Saw-Toothed Waveform

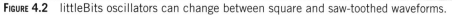

Figure 4.2   littleBits oscillators can change between square and saw-toothed waveforms.

Now that you have experimented making your oscillator sounds with your mouth, you can set up you littleBits (power, oscillator, speaker) in order to hear how square- and saw-toothed-shaped waveforms sound (Figure 4.3).

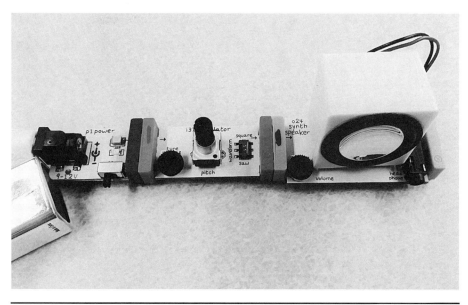

Figure 4.3   Let's play with the oscillator. Listen to the difference in the sound between square and saw-toothed wave forms.

Step Two

We are now going to move on to learn how the envelope works. Once again, take a minute or two to make your sound, this time making the movements of your mouth very slowly and then very fast.

Once you have experimented making the sounds using your mouth, take out the littleBits Envelope bit. The shape of your mouth, with your lips opening and closing in different shapes, is much like the envelope. It controls how the sound is shaped.

The Envelope bit consists of two knobs that allow you to shape your sound. The Attack controls how long it will take for your sound to reach maximum volume. The Decay controls the amount of time it takes the sound to fade out to silence.

Now you can add the Envelope bit to the littleBits chain to see how the Attack and Decay features work. Your chain will now be a Power bit, Oscillator bit, Envelope bit, and Speaker. Take some time to play around with the Envelope bit and see how it changes the sound (Figure 4.4).

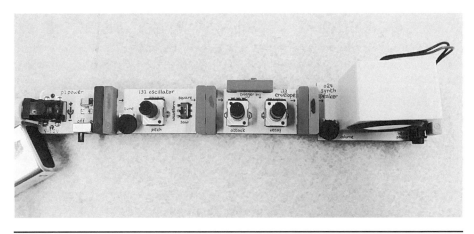

FIGURE 4.4   Let's see how adding the envelope changes the sound.

In a class setting, you will want to review Steps One and Two of the project and draw parallels between the sounds the children are making with their bodies and the Synth Kit sounds. You can also talk about which traditional instruments have fast or slow attacks and decays. For example, a slowly bowed cello has a slow attack and slow decay, meaning that the bow is drawn slowly over the strings and pulled away slowly, resulting in a sound that is slow to fade. A snare drum typically has a fast attack and decay, meaning that the drumstick hits the drum and is released quickly, resulting in a sharp sound that fades quickly. You can demonstrate these sounds to the class using the GarageBand app or real instruments if you are lucky enough to have them available. You can even use the instruments you made in Chapter 3 to see this effect as well.

Step Three

It's time to go back to the unique noises you made in Steps One and Two again. This time, cup your hands over both ears. Open and close the cover over your ears in various degrees. Experiment with this for a few minutes to hear how the sound changes as you change the way you are cupping your hands over your ears. Say, "Now you've created a filter. As you move your hands over your ears, you allow your ears to hear certain frequencies (parts of the sound) more, while lessening others" (Figures 4.5 and 4.6).

FIGURE 4.5   Let's create a human filter by opening and closing our hands over our ears.

Once again, if you are teaching a class, encourage each child to present his or her noise to the group while the rest of the kids experiment with their hands opening and closing over their ears. If you are working on your own, you can move on to working with the filter in your kit.

FIGURE 4.6   Human filter.

You are now ready to go back to the bits and add the filter to your synth. Your synth will now be composed of a Power bit, Oscillator bit, Envelope bit, Filter bit, and Speaker. The Filter bit has a big effect on the sound you have created. It can be used to make the sound "brighter" or "darker" by adjusting the knobs on the bit. The Filter bit has two knobs that affect the sound. The Cutoff will set the frequency you wish to emphasize, while the Peak controls the intensity. To make the sound brighter, you turn the knob up to emphasize the high frequencies and do the reverse to emphasize the low frequencies, making the sound darker. An interesting thing to note is that you can turn the filter into an oscillator by turning the Cutoff all the way up. Try experimenting with the filter to make your sound brighter and darker.

Step Four

Give a general review of what you've learned so far, equating the parts of the body with each bit in the kit explored in this project. Have the children build their own replica of your single-oscillator synthesizer. Remember that each Synth Kit has only enough bits to build one complete synthesizer. By this point in the project, you should have an idea of the level that each child has attained, making it an ideal point to split the kids into pairs to work with the kits.

Go around and help the children create their own unique synthesizer sound. Give each group a few minutes to experiment with tweaking the various knobs, which are called *potentiometers*. Ask them to settle on a sound, and have each child present his or her sound to the group.

Review fast and slow attacks and releases. Then ask the children to make a sound with a slow attack and a quick release. Give them a moment to practice, and then have them present the sound to the group. After each child presents his or her own sound, ask the group what each contribution sounded like.

Have the children swap kits and experiment with each other's work before presenting their unique sounds once again. Each group should have created a unique sound based on the tweaking and experimenting they did in Steps Two and Three.

Open Lab Time

If you are working on this project in a group or classroom setting, an open lab time is a great way for participants to continue to work with the Synth Kit. During our open lab times, we allow the kids time to explore and experiment with the other littleBits modules in the kit. They will have time to use the other bits and create sounds with multiple oscillators, the delay effect, and the noise generator. You may want to explain what the other bits actually do, but in our experience, the kids pick up on it quickly, and explanations have not been necessary. Instructors will have to troubleshoot signal path issues and connections.

Recording Your littleBits Synth Kit Sounds

One concern educators and librarians have about using littleBits in their makerspaces is that the participants are not able to bring their complete final project home. Documenting and showcasing creations are essential components of a good youth-centered makerspace program. One obvious way to document your makers' creations is through photos and videos shared on social media sites or your organization's website. The great thing about sound projects is the ability to record and share compositions and sounds that each creator has access to after the program. A great way to showcase your young music makers' creations and make them available for them to later download is to create a SoundCloud account.

Recording Your littleBits with Audacity

Step One

Set up your littleBits chain, and practice your sounds or musical piece before you start recording (Figure 4.7).

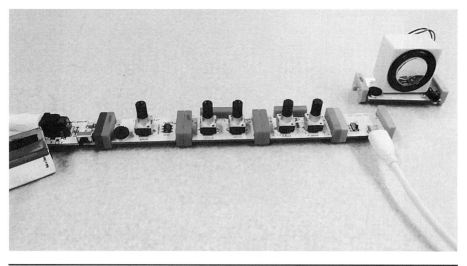

Figure 4.7   The USB I/O bit will replace the speaker in the chain when you are ready to record.

Step Two

Replace the Speaker bit with the USB I/O bit and open up Audacity or other recording software of your choice. Plug the USB into your computer (Figure 4.8).

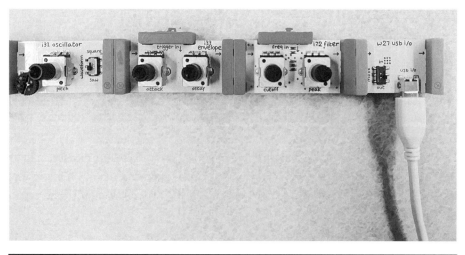

Figure 4.8   Plug the USB cable into the bit and connect to your computer to record your bits.

Step Three

Set the USB I/O bit to "Out." This will send the signal from your littleBits to your computer software.

Step Four

Open a new file, and then select Tracks > Add New > Audio Track (Figure 4.9).

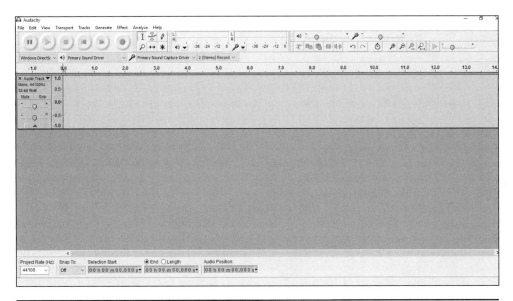

FIGURE 4.9   Open a new file in Audacity to record your bits.

Step Five

Press the red Record button, and play your sounds.

Step Six

Press the brown square Stop button, and then hit the green triangular Play button to hear your recording. You can record several tracks in the same file.

Step Seven

Under File, choose Export Audio to save your recording as an audio file rather than as an Audacity file. Under Save As Type, choose the file type you wish your recording to be. I will choose MP3. When you save your file, a pop-up box appears asking you to enter information about the song. This is called *metadata*. Enter in as much or as little information as you like (Figure 4.10).

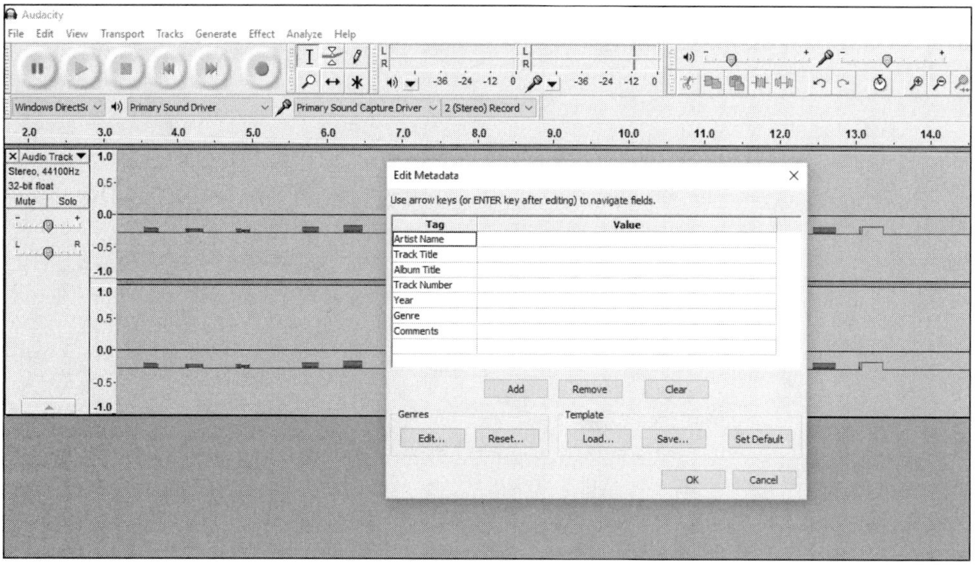

FIGURE 4.10   Enter as much information as you would like about your recording.

Step Eight

To save an MP3 file from Audacity, you will need to download the LAME MP3 Encoder software. Follow the instructions on the screen to do this if you don't already have it on your computer. Once it's installed or if your software is not locating it, go to Edit > Preferences > Library. You should be able to set the LAME MP3 Encoder that you just installed there.

Step Nine

Log in to SoundCloud, and select Upload. Click on Choose File to Upload, and select your file from your computer. Click "Open," and you will see your track uploading (Figure 4.11).

Figure 4.11 Click to upload your MP3 file.

Step Ten

You can now add an image, give your track a new title, make it public or private, and select a number of other options (Figure 4.12).

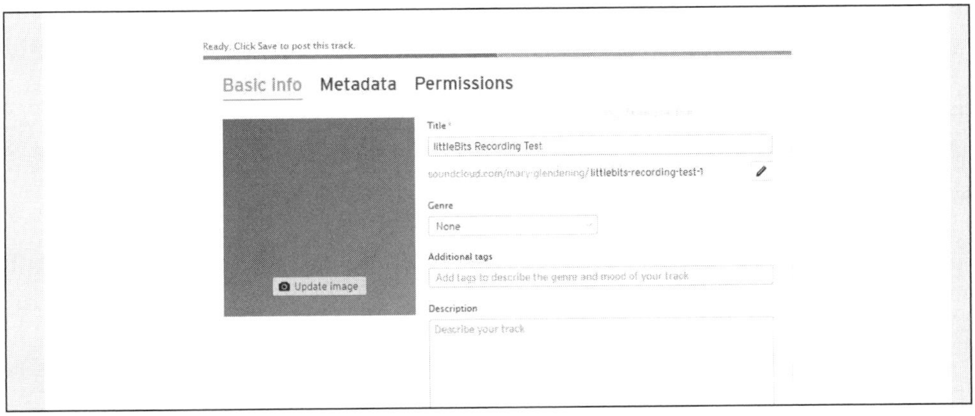

Figure 4.12 Edit the information you want to include about your track.

Now you have successfully recorded and uploaded a track to SoundCloud! Now that you have learned how you can share and save your littleBits projects, you may wish to use that knowledge gained from the hands-on lesson you just completed to move onto a digital audio workstation (DAW) or iPad to explore some of the sophisticated virtual synthesizers available. Students should be encouraged to experiment. We have had great success with children taking to the software in a familiar environment. In about an hour or more, they have gone from the equivalent of creating cave paintings to making Pixar films.

Making Beats with the iElectribe

It is often said that music is simply an artful organization of sound. While the term *artful* rings of subjectivity, the *organization* part is truly what separates music from random sounds. In the world of modern music production, this "organization" of our noise is often referred to as either *programming*, *sequencing*, or *arranging*. While we touch on sequencing with the littleBits Synth Kit in this chapter, there is a much larger world of possibility in terms of organizing sound in a musical fashion in the realm of software, more specifically, apps.

In the next project, we will meld the basics of programming the iElectribe with a basic understanding of percussion. The iElectribe app was born of the infamous Korg Electribe-R, which has found a second life in the form of an easily accessible, cost-friendly app. In fact, the app one-ups the original hardware Electribe-R drum machine by adding a whole slew of options and effects that make it a powerhouse of a production tool. You can have all of this for less than $20, making it ideal for budget-conscious programs and young/poor/starving/thrifty artists.

Materials

- Buckets and sticks (contractor's buckets and drumsticks recommended)
- iPad with iElectribe app
- Headphones
- Stereo system with ⅛-inch audio cable input (optional)
- ⅛- to ⅛-inch audio cable (optional)

Age Range and Class Size

The first part of this project works with kids of all ages, provided that they can hold a stick and bang on things with it while understanding the effect of their actions! Both parts have been successful with people from the ages of seven years and up!

Time Frame

This program can run anywhere from 60 to 90 minutes depending on the student age group and how much time for experimentation you allow.

What You Do

This project has two main parts, with the app interaction intended to be the bulk of it. However, with younger students, we have seen the first part be a fantastic exercise on its own and have allowed it to go at length for the sheer enjoyment of the kids.

You may also choose to discuss with your group the nature of percussion and the history of drum machines. We happen to own a few vintage and modern drum machines that we show from oldest to newest while we talk about their history fairly briefly. You don't have to be a massive geek about this, but it is nice to give people a little background about the instrument before diving into the project. However, Step One of this project does a good job of demonstrating percussion from a sort of caveman point of view to the ultramodern, high-tech tool used in Step Two.

Step One: Pots and Pans ... or Just a Bucket!

Explain the nature of various sounds and textures and their outcome. Hold the bucket between your knees, bottom up, and slap it lightly and quickly. Discuss the nature of the sound it makes, and have the kids try on their own. Then slap the bucket again but slowly, and leave your hand on it for a fraction longer, indicating to the children the difference in the sound—showing that the first sound had a higher pitch and the latter had more of a low, bassy thud.

Do the same with the sticks, with the students now striking various spots on the bucket and in different positions. Try placing the bottom of the bucket down on the floor and tapping lightly on the handle or rim for higher pitches, and have your students experiment with this as well. You may even go so far as to put pillows in the buckets and use wider "drumsticks" (i.e., rulers). Make sure to note how the pitch, attack (start), and release (end) of the sound changes as the stick meets different parts (textures) of the bucket and even changes with the velocity (speed and power) of the various hits. For example, tapping the handle lightly and fast causes a higher-pitched percussive sound reminiscent of a cymbal, whereas slapping it with an open palm causes a thud much like a bass drum of an acoustic drum kit.

Step Two: Building a Beat

Let your students experiment with this activity, and encourage them to build a beat (explained as a sequence). As often suggested in this text, the instructor should feel free to do these types of exercises along with the students and take moments to pause and help them out or showcase what they are working on. Gauging the maturity of the group (age isn't always a determining factor), you may want to have a longer "experimentation" portion before zoning them in to construct an actual beat.

After you feel that your students have come to a good point where they can show off what they made, have each one "solo" what he or she has come up on. If time permits, have them discuss their findings afterward. The key is to keep the solo fast paced so that no one loses what he or she had come up with. Also, take a moment to reflect on what people came up with and the various methods they used to make the sounds with which they composed their beats/sequences.

You may go one step further and set an Init patch (blank program with a simple quarter-note kick drum pattern) on the iElectribe up through an amplification source (i.e., stereo system via the ⅛-inch jacks), and have your students build a sequence as a group, where all the students line up with their bucket drums next to each other and hit the drums however they choose on the beat in order, thus building a human drum machine!

Step Three: Kids Build Their Own Beat and Share

This can be a bit much depending on age and memory. Gauge your audience and have success with younger patrons with the following scheme. As they play, make it a game like *freeze tag*, where the rules call on one person to act, and everyone else goes quiet and listens to what that kid is building. Go around the room at intervals, and call on each one to perform. It is helpful to tinker alongside them and show your own beat or sequence off from time to time. As with most projects in this book, be prepared for things to get LOUD!

Step Four: Show the App

Have your students open the app, select an Init patch, and spend a few moments experimenting and discovering what the app is capable of (Figure 4.13).

Draw the children's focus to the individual sound buttons and demonstrate what each one does. From there, go one to having students pick one sound and use the various sound-shaping tools to alter it. For the sake of being brief, and for the simple matter that an entire book could be written about those features alone, make sure to keep the focus tight and allow students to experiment within a reasonable time frame.

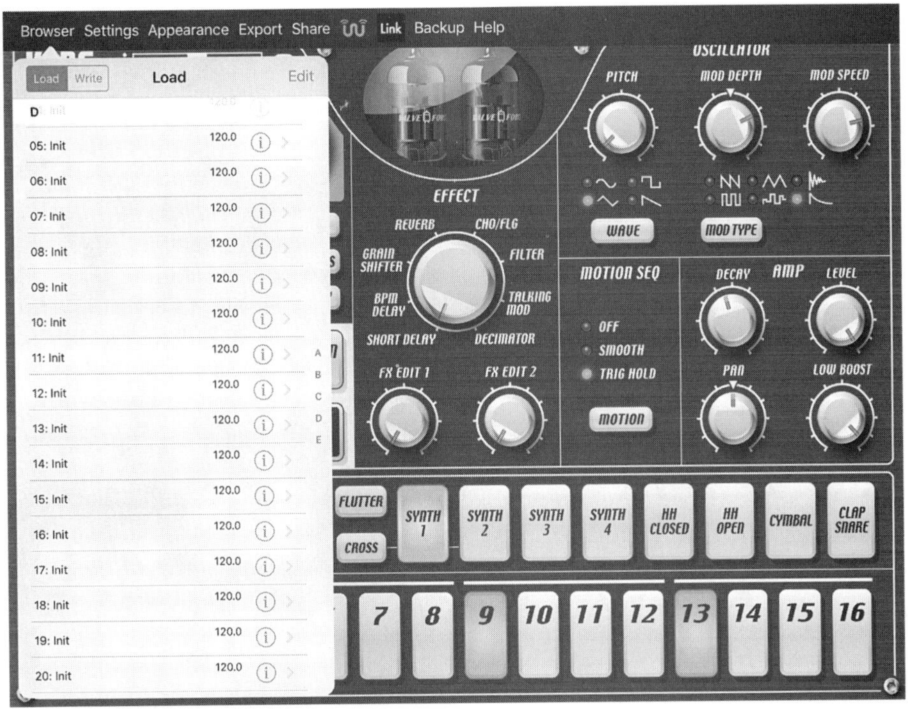

Figure 4.13 Select an INIT patch to get started.

Demonstrate to the students that the 16 buttons at the bottom light up green in sequence when played, and for each drum they choose, students have the option of highlighting a number in the sequence, turning that button to red, which will then trigger that sound when played.

Step Five: Sequencing Time!

Have your students redo the Init step again. Select the Kick, and "turn off" the kick before proceeding by selecting the Kick first and then hitting the corresponding red triggers in the following sequence. Give your students a hand building the sequence once they are ready.

- Kick: 1-5-9-13
- HH closed: 4-7-8-11-12-15
- HH open: 3-7-11-15
- Clap Snare: 5-13
- Synth(3): 1-2-9-11
- Synth(4): 5-10-13

Build this groove with the class by having them hit the individual drum sound and then the corresponding number on the sequencer at the lower part of the screen (Figures 4.14 and 4.15).

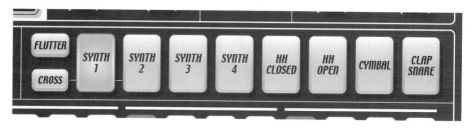

Figure 4.14   Select a drum button to select a drum sound.

Figure 4.15   Build your sequence.

Take a moment to go around and check each student. You may have the students experiment from there, once they are all set, or ...

Step Six: Reset (Init) and Experiment

Before you begin, show your students the Tempo setting by selecting that button and moving the wheel icon to the right of it. Explain that this gives them the option of having the sequences they create play faster or slower. Then have your students go back to an Init file and build their own sequences. This may take the bulk of your time and is the intent of the project here, so please plan accordingly.

Step Seven: Name Your Project and Share!

Have your students name and share their projects with the class by jacking into any available amplification system you have access to. Encourage the students to explain how they made their sounds and what genre of music their creation could fit into!

Making Sound with Scratch and Makey Makey

Makey Makey is a very popular tool in makerspaces probably because it has so many uses and can be used in a wide variety of projects. We won't spend too much time with the Makey Makey because there is already a wide body of tutorials and projects out there, but we would be remiss if we did not introduce this fun and easy-to-use tool.

The Makey Makey can turn everyday items into a controller for your computer, allowing you to use such things as Play-Doh, pencil drawings, fruit, aluminum foil, and more as the mouse and keys. This basic functioning allows you to use the Makey Makey with a variety of software and websites. For this project, we're going to combine the Makey Makey with Scratch to build a song. You will figure out what items you are going to use to work with the Makey Makey and then build the program in Scratch that you will use to build your song.

To get started, create an account on Scratch by visiting http://scratch.mit.edu. Click on Join Scratch, and create your account. After you have created your account, click on Create to get started with your project. When your new project opens, you will see the Scratch work area. On the left is the Stage, in the middle are the command blocks, and on the right is your project building area (Figure 4.16).

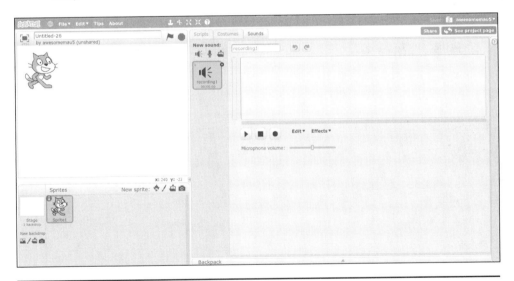

Figure 4.16   The Scratch workspace.

For this project, we don't really need to worry about the Stage area because we are not going to be creating animations. To get started, choose your sounds by clicking on the Sound tab in the middle section of the screen. This will open the area where you can record your own sounds, upload sounds from your computer, or choose for the included sound boards. For this project, we will choose sounds from the sound library. Clicking on the speaker icon will open the sound library (Figures 4.17 and 4.18).

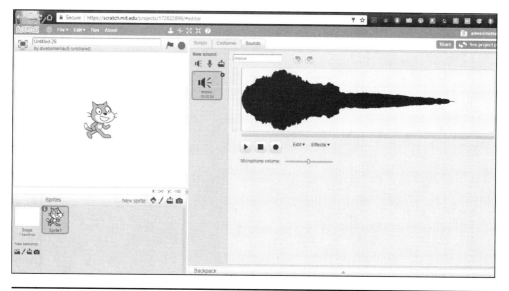

FIGURE 4.17   Click on Sounds to open the Sound tools.

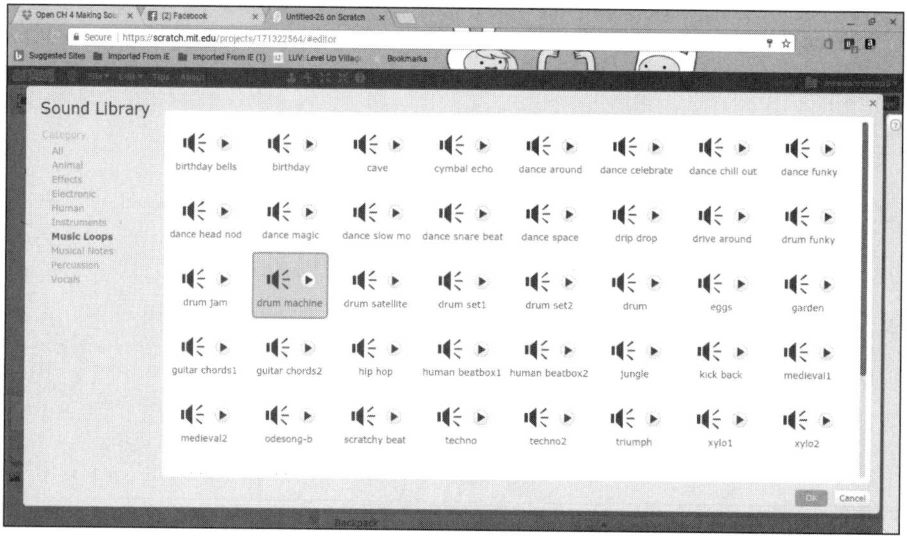

FIGURE 4.18   The Sound Library offers a variety of sounds for your projects.

Play around with the sounds, listening to various instruments and beats. You can choose to use a single note such as the Electric Bass-C, or you can choose music loops or any combination you wish. Think about what you would like the user of your creation to be able to do, or perhaps you are looking to build an "electric" bass out of cardboard and other recycled materials. Once you have decided on a sound you wish to use, select the sound to highlight it, and click on OK to add it to your personal sound library (Figure 4.19).

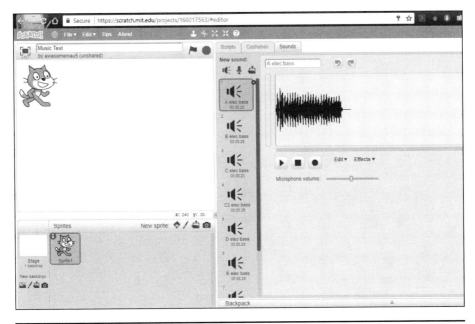

Figure 4.19 You will see your selections from the Sound Library in the middle of the screen.

Select all the sounds you want to use for your project. Once you have selected them, you can personalize them a bit via editing in the Scratch program. As you can see, you can edit the sound by cutting, copying, and pasting or by adding effects. To edit the sound, click on the part of the sound wave that you want to edit, and then choose the effect or edit option you want to use. In this example, I have chosen to reverse a portion of the sound (Figures 4.20 and 4.21).

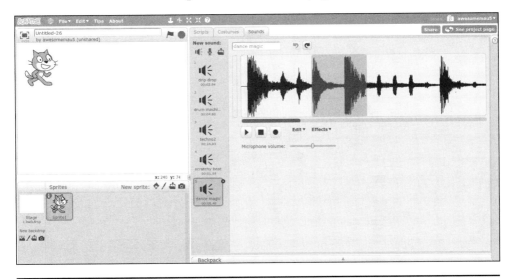

Figure 4.20   Select the portion of the sound you wish to change.

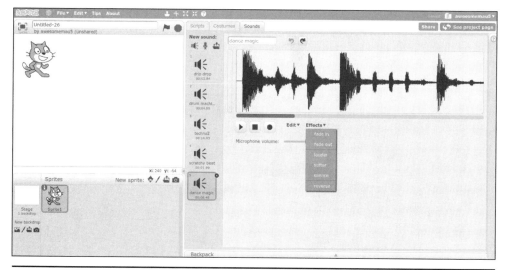

FIGURE 4.21   Click on the way you wish to edit the sound in the pull-down selection list.

Once you have selected your sounds and edited them to sound the way you like, you are ready to work with the Makey Makey. Click on Scripts at the top of the middle portion of the Scratch work area. For this project, we're going to work with Events and Sounds. To get started, choose the block that says "When Space Key Pressed." You will notice a little down arrow next to the word "Space." This opens a pull-down menu that allows you to assign a sound to a specific action (Figure 4.22).

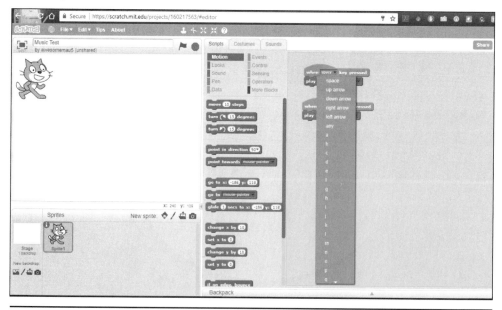

FIGURE 4.22   Assign each event to a corresponding "key" on the Makey Makey.

Move the command block over to the work area. You can move over as many of these command blocks as you will need for your project now, or you can switch back and forth between command block selections. Once you have moved over the number of command blocks you wish to use, you're ready to work with the Sound blocks (Figure 4.23).

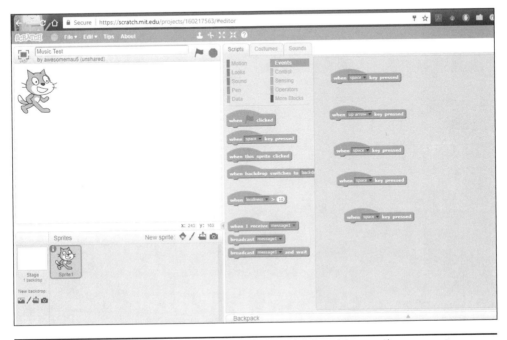

Figure 4.23   Move over the number of commands you wish to set to save time.

You have some choices as to how you want to work with the sounds. You can simply pull over the block "Play Sound XXX Until Done," setting up a sound to play when a particular key on your keyboard is touched. Be sure to know what keys can be "programmed" on the Makey Makey. Don't forget to give your project a name so that you can find it in your projects file later (Figure 4.24).

Now that you have your project set up in Scratch, you are ready to start working with the Makey Makey. If you don't have a Makey Makey, you can still have fun experimenting with creating a song with the sounds you've chosen using your computer's keyboard. As mentioned previously, the Makey Makey works with any object that can carry a charge and any software or Internet site that uses a mouse and keyboard commands. The computer cannot tell if you are touching the space key or a piece of fruit, but the Makey Makey makes it so that the computer "thinks" you are touching the space key on the keyboard (Figure 4.25).

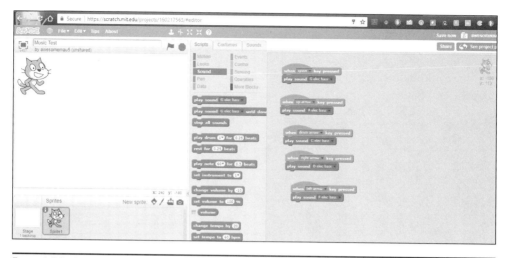

FIGURE 4.24   Your completed Scratch program should look something like this.

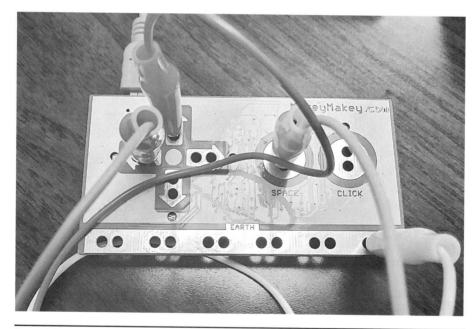

FIGURE 4.25   Connect your alligator clips to the Makey Makey and the project pieces. The alligator clips correspond to keys on the keyboard and mouse.

Now that you have a basic understanding of how the Makey Makey works, it's time to design the physical part of your project. You may wish to repurpose one of the instruments you made in Chapter 3 to now become your Makey Makey instrument. Perhaps I crafted a guitar out of a cereal box and paper tube. I can now add a few extra touches to make it an electric bass that will play bass sounds. To make my instrument more realistic, I can even model it off the open strings on the neck of a bass guitar. Another fun idea would be to draw a design on a piece of paper with a pencil or conductive ink. If you use a pencil, a No. 2B works really well. If you are working on this project in a group, put out craft supplies as well as such things as copper tape, aluminum foil, and so on that can be used to trigger the Makey Makey. Students can take a look at the supplies available to them to get ideas as to what kind of sound project they want to build in with the real-world materials and then go back to Scratch to create and choose the sounds they want for their project (Figure 4.26).

FIGURE 4.26   Here's my completed project!

CHAPTER 5

Recording Sound

Now that you have a bit of sound-creation experience under your belt, this is a good time to learn how to record and manipulate the sounds you create. Through these hands-on projects, you will have fun learning how to record sound using a variety of tools along with understanding the various ways to control and manipulate the physics of sound before and after recording sound.

Acoustics: Sound in Space and Time!

This section involves teaching the fundamental science behind what are known as *time-based effects* in audio engineering (see www.sweetwater.com/insync/time -based-effect/). There are three fundamental methods of signal processing, but perhaps the most obvious and translatable to people of all ages lies in an understanding of acoustics: how space relates to the recording and transmission of sound. As with our percussion project, we find that different materials, sizes, densities, and the manner in which we generate sounds with them are linked. The physics of sound in relation to space and time, as you will see, can be elaborated on greatly depending on just how creative you decide to get! You will be able to understand the importance of our environment and how it affects sound with this project. Simply put, you are going to dive into the realm of that lovely effect known as *reverb*.

Materials

- *Reverb*. Various spaces (i.e., bathroom/shower, between three pillows, outdoors). Get ready to change locations and pull out various found objects from the kitchen, depending on how far you wish to take the lesson.
- *Recording/playback device (iPad/phone/tablet/laptop with audio interface and mic)*. The sophistication of the devices and software is scalable, and the overall lesson should prove true regardless of the equipment used.

Age Range and Class Size

This project can be done in small groups or solo. Whether you go "into the field" alone to make these recordings or with a small group, it is key that the sounds being made and recorded are fairly consistent because that will help to demonstrate the lesson in play here.

Time Frame

This project can be as long or as short as you wish, taking more time depending on the locations and materials you choose. Provided below is a very simple version, but it is easy to see how things can get a bit involved if you choose to vary the materials and locations.

What You Do

Most smartphones and tablet devices have a "voice memo" or recording app preinstalled. If you can't locate one, there is a good selection of freeware apps available on the web. If you have a more elaborate setup such as a laptop with an audio interface and condenser mic, that will work better, but such complexity is not necessary.

Pick a word or phrase to speak and percussive sound to make using any simple tools. A phrase such as "Oh yeah!" and clapping your hands in a slow rhythm to record for the project will bring consistent success. Do not feel limited by this suggestion, and change it any way you want. You could make clicking sounds with your mouth and/or sing a phrase from your favorite song.

Step One: Tiny Recording Booth

It's time to make a pillow fort! Take four cushions or pillows (couch pillows or cushions work best). You will need these to make the walls and ceiling for your little recording booth and be able to fit your recording device and sound-making items inside.

Once you've set up your booth, record the voice phrase and the more percussive noise you have chosen (Figure 5.1).

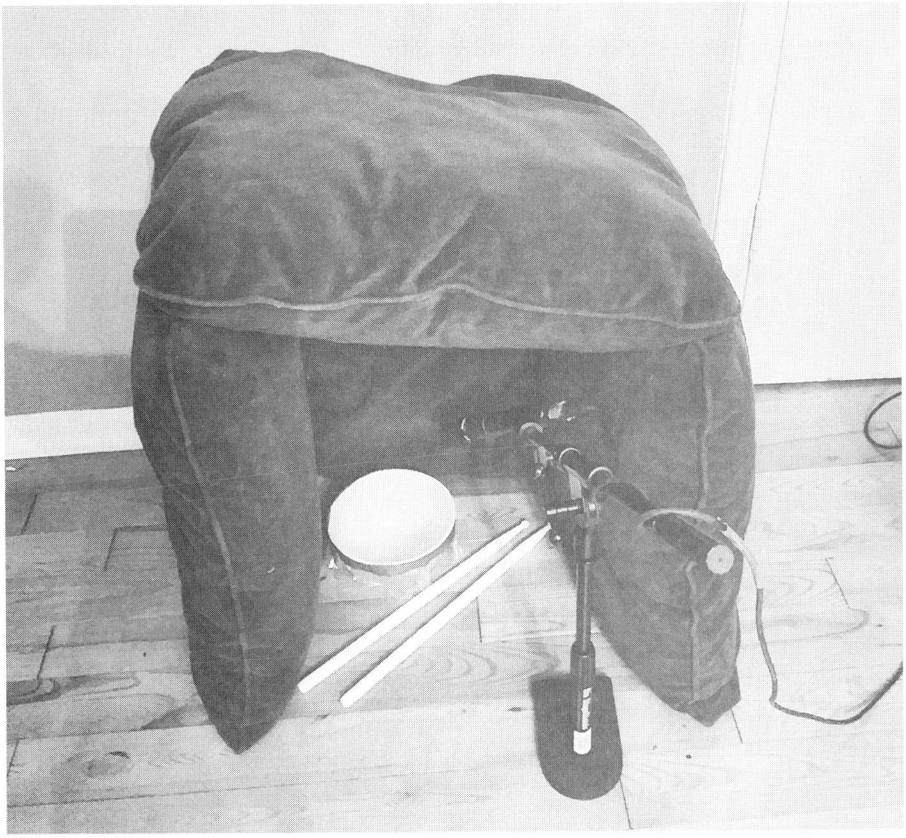

Figure 5.1   Build a fort out of pillows or cushions.

Step Two: Hit the Showers!

Take your recording setup to a bathroom or shower room, any place with tiles should do but isn't 100 percent necessary. Try to place your recording in the center of the room, and take a few steps back. Then make a second pair of recordings with those two sounds closer to a wall.

Now that you have that set up, record that same voice phrase and percussive sound. You have to raise the volume of the phrase depending on the type of recording setup you have. If you have a decently sophisticated microphone and audio recording setup, raise the gain a little, and perform the two sounds as you did in the first part of this project. If you are using something as simple as an app on a phone, play the sounds a little louder. Experiment to find the right volume.

What you should notice in the recordings between the first and second locations is that there will be more reverb on the recordings in Step Two. Step One was recorded in close proximity, in a space with materials that absorb sound rather than reflect it. The reflected sounds cause what is known as *reverb*.

What should also become apparent is the whole space and time aspect in this second set of recordings. The closer the sound is recorded to a wall versus the center of the room, the greater will be the reverb. This is the time factor playing a part in the difference between less time and more time for the sounds to be reflected off the nearby surfaces. causing a change in the feel of the reverb at play.

Step Three: Let's Take It One, Two, Maybe Three Steps Further

If you have the tools, take the recordings from Steps One and Two and import them into any digital audio workstation (DAW) software (e.g., GarageBand or Cubase) and experiment with adding a reverb effect to the first recording in order to make it sound more like the second recording. All of these apps include reverb plug-ins that vary in sophistication and control.

You will notice that depending on the sophistication of the software, you will gain control over a few aspects that help you to emulate an environment. Often these apps have presets with names such as "hall" and "bathroom" for obvious reasons. Some of these plug-ins even allow you to control the various types of surfaces (e.g., tile, drywall, and stone), their distance from the recorded source, where they are in the room, and the density of the materials in your simulated environment.

You may even opt to skip all that completely, go back to Step One, and change the materials that make up your recording booth or take your recording setup to different spaces such as an empty hall, an elevator, or wherever you can execute the projects safely. Another way to get a little more experimental with your recordings is by creating them inside other objects. You might opt to place your recording device inside a large box or metal bowl. The possibilities are limited only by your resources and imagination.

Delay: Laser Machine and Microphone

Delay in the audio production world is a form of processing that is sometimes referred to as an *echo effect*. Like reverb, delay is a time-based process where the source sound is reflected and repeated to some degree. You may choose to experiment with the Delay bit in the littleBits Synth Kit if you have one or go a more organic, cost-effective route with the following project. The delay effect with this project may not be as dramatic as those found in the various apps we discuss in this book but can be a lot of fun and gives you a fun way to create unique sounds such as those used in older science fiction films.

Materials

- *Slinky*. Yes! That old favorite toy from yesteryear will be our main tone generator in this project. You can find it in most dollar stores and toy stores as well as some department stores.
- *Plastic cup*. Preferably a large, disposable beverage cup such as the kind you would find at a party. Styrofoam will not work as well, but a plastic drink cup that is fairly sturdy will definitely do the trick.
- *Adhesive or binding material*. A hot glue gun could work, but we have had success with strong tape, paperclips, popsicle sticks, and even small amounts of string. It all depends on how far and how permanent you want your creation to be!

Age Range and Class Size

This project, in our experience, has worked with children as young as six years old. Keep in mind that the materials available and the ability of the students will dictate how much one-on-one assistance is required. Our tween and teen groups have had success with this fairly quickly after being shown a prototype and have taken the project in interesting directions by adding materials or putting the project inside other environments such as those in the preceding project.

Time Frame

This project usually takes anywhere from 30 to 60 minutes based on the age of those engaging in it and the materials available.

What You Do

It is helpful to have the finished project assembled first to show the group what they will be making. Having a variety of cup and Slinky sizes has also made the project enjoyable and more of a unique experience for those who have worked on it.

Take a cup, place a Slinky inside of it at the base, and turn it upside down. By tapping on the Slinky or the cup (depending on the materials), you can produce a resonant, delayed after-effect of the initial tap. Tapping on the Slinky as it hangs out at various spots will produce a variation of that effect (Figures 5.2 and 5.3).

FIGURE 5.2   Cut a hole in the bottom of the cup to make it easier to attach the Slinky.

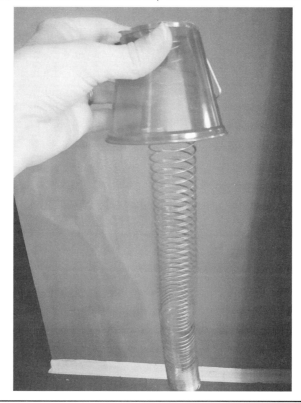

FIGURE 5.3   You are now ready to create laser sound effects!

One Step Further

Fix the other end of the Slinky to the open end of the cup so that the toy maintains its upright, cylindrical shape. Speak into it. If you have a number of Slinky and cup sizes, this will produce a variety of interesting effects (Figure 5.4).

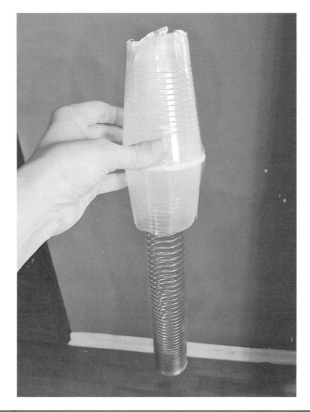

FIGURE 5.4   You can also use two cups to see if the sound changes.

Options

You may even opt to go further with this and use elements such as PVC pipe, which can be found in cheap supply at any hardware store, and cap one end. Various longer lengths and widths of pipe will make the effect far more dramatic for both steps of this project (Figures 5.5 and 5.6).

FIGURE 5.5   You can use a PVC pipe with a Slinky inside to experiment further.

FIGURE 5.6   Tap the Slinky to hear the differnce in sound.

Basic Sampling

Sampling, when boiled down to a simple definition, is basically recording a sound and playing it back via a trigger (i.e., a keyboard). Sampling technology has become sophisticated to the point where a composer can command what sounds like a highly realistic orchestra with the use of some sampling hardware or software. The more sophisticated the sampler, the greater control one has over the sounds one records or loads into the sampler via multiple formats from myriad vendors.

Due to the popularity of sampling and the great variety of samplers available, we will keep it quite simple and highly affordable with this project. Keezy is a lovely bit of freeware (free software) that allows just about anyone to record or "sample" from their smartphones or tablets. While limited in its editing capabilities, Keezy does hit the spot with recording and playback via a very colorful interface.

Find It, Pitch It, Sample It!

Here you will experiment with basic sampling technology to create a sampled instrument with a variety of pitches.

Materials

- *Glass bottle*. Grab a bottle to be filled with liquid. The larger the bottle, the better. Bottles made of other materials will also work, but we have found greater success with glass or metal containers. The greater the bottle in circumference and length, the more dramatic the project will be.
- *Liquid*. Water is bountiful and free. You may choose to use another liquid, and the outcome will be different depending on the density of the liquid. This project will also work great with laundry detergent.
- *Hard surface*. We suggest that you use a hard, level surface for this project. A hardwood or (large panel) tile floor is optimal but not necessary.
- *Device with Keezy software*. This can be an iPad, iPod, or iPhone. At this time Keezy is only available for iOS. If you are using a laptop or Android device you will need to use a different sampling app. If you choose to use another piece of sampling software, please see the note at the end of this project.

Age Range and Class Size

This is certainly a project for small groups (two to three people), but it certainly can be executed by a single person. Silent communication will be key between the members of the group so that the recordings can be pure in terms of capturing the sounds they will be recording. Depending on the maturity of the group, this is feasible for most age groups but recommended for tweens and teens.

Time Frame

Depending on how complex or creative you get, this project could easily take an hour or more to execute.

What You Do

Set up your device on the floor, and mark a "starting line" close to the mic input. Make sure that this is a fixed position for all the recordings. If you are doing this in a small group, be aware that any unwanted sounds will corrupt the process/ recording. It is highly advised that members of the group take a few test runs and use quiet signals such as hand gestures to communicate while recording each step.

Part One

Step One
In Keezy, use the bottom-left pad (purple if in portrait mode), and record the bottle rolling from just behind the starting line for the duration of Keezy's allowed recording time per pad (Figure 5.7).

Step Two
Fill one-quarter of your bottle with liquid, and repeat Step One (Figure 5.8).

Figure 5.7   Mark a starting line near your iPad with the Keezy app ready to go.

Figure 5.8   Start out with your bottle filled 1/4 of the way with water.

Step Three

Fill half the bottle with liquid, and repeat Step One (Figure 5.9).

FIGURE 5.9   Next fill your bottle half way and sample the sound.

Step Four

Fill the whole bottle with liquid, and repeat Step One (Figure 5.10).

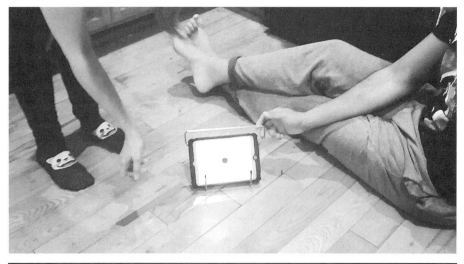

FIGURE 5.10   Fill the bottle all the way and make your third recording.

As we discussed in Chapter 4 with regard to Envelope, this sound should produce a hard attack and slow release because the sound will sort of "fade out" while the bottle rolls away from the mic input. You will have four distinct pitches from the same sound and will have created a sampled, pitched instrument all your own.

Part Two

Experiment and change the shape of your new instrument. One way we suggest is to move the recording device with mic input, or physical mic if you choose to use one, to a fixed position further from the starting line and repeat the process from Steps One through Four. You will likely find a softer attack or "fade-in" of the sound as well as release. You can make the release shorter by either physically stopping the bottle or cutting the recording short. We recommend using something soft at the other end such as a paperback book taped down to stop the rolling motion without breaking things.

One Step Further

You can take this one step further by filling the bottles with other objects or creating a variety of textured sounds by adding other objects to the bottle and using a more dense liquid (e.g., a suspension). There are many variables involved in this project. Once participants have the basic version of the project down, they should feel free to alter the variables. One suggestion is to keep the recording input in a fixed spot for consistency in terms of general playback volume and the envelope of the sounds.

NOTE: *If you choose to not go the Keezy route and use a more sophisticated sampler, we suggest that you find a way to identify the pitches of your recordings and map them accordingly across the keyboard, sampling your instrument every three semitones (keys). While a lot of the software available these days can take one recording and spread it across various octaves for playback, they can sound a bit artificial beyond a certain range. This is actually kind of cool! Experiment! Have fun!*

CHAPTER 6

Beyond the Basics or Putting It All Together

This chapter will take what we learned in previous chapters to create projects using techniques and tools that bring together audio and other skills.

Bare Conductive Touch Board Project

A Bare Conductive Touch Board is a great tool for a variety of interactive music and sound-based projects. The Touch Board can be used as an MP3 player, and you can reprogram it to use as a MIDI controller as well as to program with an Arduino. The possibilities for projects using this board are really endless.

While Bare Conductive makes a special conductive ink that you can use to create murals and other interactive projects, you can also use other conductive materials with the Touch Board. You can easily create an interactive quilt or clothing project using conductive thread. Copper tape is another conductive medium that is great for connecting your board to a trigger, especially if you want to create a long distance between the board and the trigger. Alligator clips, aluminum foil, really, any conductive material will work with the board.

Before we get started with the project, you will need to get familiar with the board. Starting at the top of the Touch Board and working our way down, here are the parts of the board you will be working with for this project (Figure 6.1):

- *Touch sensor/electrodes.* These sensors (E0–E11) can be connected to electric paint, conductive thread, copper tape, or any other conductive material. When they are touched, your sound will play.
- *Speaker/headphone jack.*

- *MicroSD card reader.* The SD card comes preprogrammed with a Touch Board tutorial. Remove the microSD card and replace the tutorial with your own sounds.
- *USB mini.* Plug a mini USB cord into your computer or a wall adapter to power your board. You can also reprogram the board by plugging it into your computer.
- *3.7-V LiPo battery charger.* You can also power your board using a 3.7-V lithium-polymer (LiPo) battery if you don't wish to have a cord as part of your project.
- *On/off switch.*
- *Reset button.* Push this button to recalibrate the sensors when you load a new project on your microSD card.

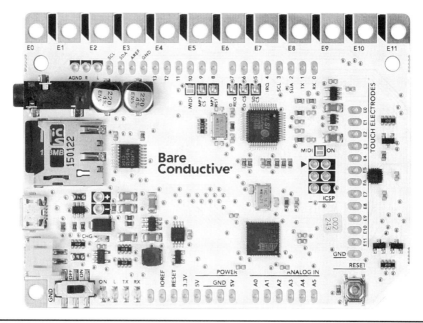

FIGURE 6.1   The Bare Conductive Touch Board works with all kinds of conductive materials. *Bare Conductive Touch Board and photo provided by Bare Conductive.*

Getting Started with the Bare Conductive Touch Board

For this beginner's project, we are going to take a folk tale or tall tale to create an interactive storytelling experience. We will use the story of John Henry, which I selected because it's not only a great story but also has a lot of opportunities to create sound effects to use at key points in the story. When selecting a story for your project, you'll want to read it through a few times and think about the sounds you can use to enhance the story. You may wish to take notes and write down your ideas for the sounds you will use in your project. This list will help you as you find the sounds to use in your project and start to record.

Sounds for Interactive John Henry Story Board

- Ooohs and aaahs of animals and birds when they meet baby John Henry
- Evil laugh of Ferret-Faced Freddy
- Gunshot at the beginning of the race
- Explosion of dynamite
- Ring of John Henry's hammer
- Boulders or rocks falling
- Steam engine
- People yelling "John Henry"
- Soft crying
- Clapping or applause

There are several ways you can get the sounds to use in this project. If you have the equipment to record audio, you will want to use the skills from previous chapters to try your hand at recording your own sounds. As you can see from the preceding list, you may need to get creative to find the right sound effect as well as to record the voice. You will want to record each sound as a separate file and save the files in the MP3 format. Unlike the LilyPad MP3 device, the Touch Board can only play MP3 files. If you are having trouble recording a sound you want or unhappy with the results, you can find royalty-free sound effects to incorporate into your project on the web.

Sources for Royalty-Free Sound Effects

- *Soundbible.com.* This site has an easily searchable database of sounds for use in your projects. Files can be downloaded in MP3 or WAV format.
- *Freesound* (http://freesound.org). Freesound is a collaborative collection of creative commons licensed sounds. Sound files are in a variety of formats, and you will need to check the file type in the information box on the right-hand side of the screen for the sound in which you are interested.

Once you have all your sounds recorded and have obtained the extra sounds you need from one of the royalty-free sound libraries, you are ready to prepare the files to load onto the microSD card that came with your Touch Board. As I mentioned previously, the files need to be in MP3 format, so any files you have that are in another file format must be converted to MP3 before you can proceed. You can do this in a variety of ways depending on the equipment you are using.

Converting a WAV to MP3 in Audacity

If you are using Audacity, you can easily convert a WAV file to MP3. First, you will need to import your file into the software by clicking on File > Import > Audio. Select the file you wish to convert to MP3 and once it is open in the software click on Export. You can now say your file in the MP3 format for use in your project. If you don't have access to a DAW program such as Audacity, you can also use an online converter to handle your files. You may need to use a web-based option if you have recorded sounds using a smartphone's built-in microphone feature because the file type may not be recognized by your software. For example, when I recorded a sample using my Android phone's microphone, the file is saved as a 3GP format. A free file converter such as Convertio (https://convertio.co/) will handle your files and quickly convert them to MP3 for you.

Now that you have your files ready to go, you will need to have your project mapped out and properly named files so that the correct one plays when you touch the painted trigger. If you have not done so already, eject the microSD card from the Touch Board and insert it into a microSD card adapter so that it can be inserted into your computer (Figure 6.2).

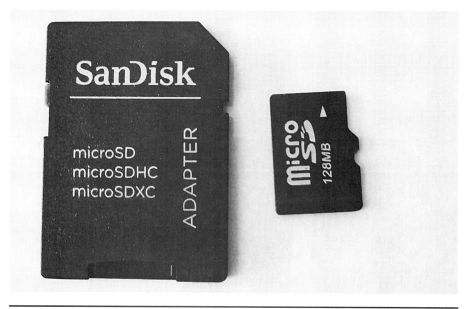

Figure 6.2   You will need a MicroSD card adapter to put files on the card.

1. Insert the adapter into the slot for the SD card in your computer. You will see the card on your computer as TB AUDIO.

2. Open the SD card. You will see a list of files on the card, including 12 files with file names of TRACK000.mp3, TRACK001.mp3, etc. These are the tutorial tracks that came preloaded on your Touch Board. You may wish to save these for future reference, which you can do by creating a new folder and moving the tracks to that new folder.

3. Rename your project files using the TRACK000.mp3, TRACK001.mp3, scheme for as many tracks as you will be using for your project. The John Henry project uses 10 tracks, so the last track file is titled TRACK009.mp3. Once your tracks are renamed, copy them to the Touch Board microSD card. Eject the card from the computer, remove it from the adapter, and place it back in the slot on your Touch Board.

4. Test to be sure your tracks are working by turning on your Touch Board. The board can be powered by plugging the microUSB cord into the Touch Board and then either plugging it into your computer or into a USB charger. Once your Touch Board is plugged in, turn the power switch to the ON position. You should see a small green light come on (Figure 6.3).

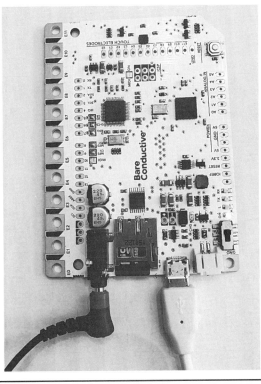

Figure 6.3 Turn on your Touch Board to get started.

5. Test your files by plugging your headphones or speakers into the audio jack. Then you can use your finger to touch the nodes that contain your sound files.

Troubleshooting

- You may need to reset your Touch Board to recalibrate it to the new files you have put on the microSD card. To reset, click the Reset button on the bottom of the board opposite the power switch. You will see the orange light flash on next to the power switch while your board resets. Once the light stops flashing, your board is ready, and you can repeat item five above.
- If resetting the Touch Board doesn't work, eject the microSD card, place it in the adapter, and plug into your computer. Check that you have properly named the files using the TRACK000.mp3 through TRACK0011.mp3 format. You will also want to be sure that you placed the tutorial files into a separate file.

Creating Your Conductive Mural

Now that you have your audio files ready, and they are working with your Touch Board, you are ready to start painting and creating your mural. For the John Henry story, we're going to use a 16- × 24-inch canvas so that you can easily transport the storyboard and mount it on a wall or place it on an easel to use in a storytelling program. You can paint on a wall or other sturdy material depending on where you would like to create your project and if you wish for it be a permanent or temporary piece.

To start, you will need to figure out the layout of your mural; as in the conductive sewing projects, you can sketch out your design plan. Just like sewing with conductive thread, you need to make sure that your paths from the board to the sensor don't cross or your project will not work. Once you have an idea of how you are going to place the sensors, you can start painting your design (Figure 6.4).

To paint your design, you can draw the design on the surface and then paint it in. You also could create stencils for a neater look. Bare Conductive makes it easy to get started with your stencil design by providing free project templates. You can use these as a place to start in designing your own. If you have access to a Silhouette cutter, you can design the stencil in the Silhouette software and set the machine to cut the stencil out of clear craft plastic. The Silhouette design store is a good place to find designs that can tie in with your project, making it even easier to create a stencil for your project (Figure 6.5).

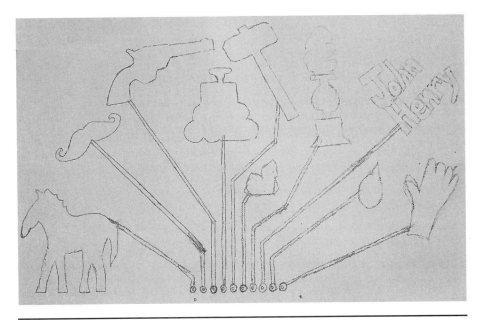

Figure 6.4 Sketch out your design on the material you will be using before you start painting.

Figure 6.5 Using stencils is a great way to get a clean finished design.

The Bare Conductive electric paint comes in a 10-milliliter tube as well as a 50-milliliter tub. For painting large designs, the tub works great, and you may find it easier to paint the lines from the Touch Board to your trigger with the tube of electric paint. The electric paint in the tub is quite thick, and you may find it difficult to work with at its normal consistency. The electric paint is water based, so you can dilute it. However, if you do, it becomes less conductive, so you want to be careful how much you dilute it. You can experiment with the dilution of the paint by mixing a few different ratios of water to paint. Be sure to label the ratio of paint to water on each container and paint a few test lines to see how it works, including a line of paint that has not been diluted with water. To test resistance in your solutions, wait for the paint to dry, and use a multimeter set to ohms to measure the resistance of your test strips. You will see that the more you have diluted the paint solution, the greater will be the resistance because the conductive particles in the paint are now spread out, and they make less contact with each other. You can experiment with painting several layers of the diluted solution on top of each other to decrease the resistance and make it easier for the paint to carry current.

Things to Keep in Mind When Painting Your Design

- You can attach the Touch Board by using the electric paint. While the paint is still wet, place your board onto the project; be sure that you painted a small circle under the place where the holes under E0 and E11 are located on the Board (Figure 6.6).
- Sensors can be any shape, but the size of your sensor will make a difference. A small sensor will respond quite easily to touch, whereas a larger sensor is better suited as a proximity sensor that will detect an object that is nearby and respond.
- Electric paint can have a slow response. This is especially true with very large sensors.
- The sensor is designed to have a trace between it and the electrodes of about 30 centimeters maximum. If you are making a large mural or want a long distance between the electrodes and your sensors, you will need to use a more conductive material such as copper tape.
- The paint needs to be dry to work, so you will need a little patience. It takes about 15 minutes for the paint to dry. Be sure that it's completely dry before testing or touching the sensors (Figure 6.7).

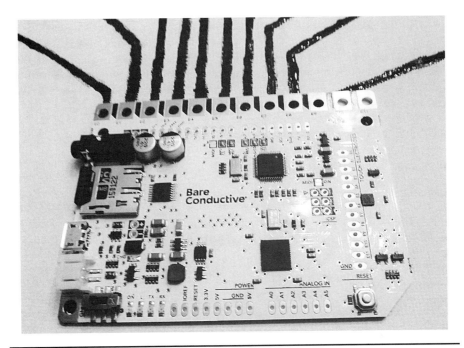

Figure 6.6   You can attach your Touch Board with the conductive paint.

Figure 6.7   Be sure the paint is completely dry, then share your story with an audience!

Troubleshooting Your Finished Project

The biggest problem you will face with this project is that a sensor does not trigger a sound when touched. Here are some things to check if you don't hear anything when you touch your sensors:

- First, you want to make sure that your electric paint is completely dry; otherwise, the sensors may not work.
- Make sure that your line from the sensor to your trigger is solid all the way to the trigger; if you have gaps or see white in your design, paint over the area again to be sure that you have enough paint with no empty space to carry the charge from your design to the sensor on the Touch Board.
- Remove the microSD card, and double-check that you have labeled the files properly and that the files actually play the sound.
- Is the path from your Touch Board to your painted sensor clear, not touching any of the other sensor paths or another sensor on the board? If your sensors or paths are touching, or if your path from the board touches another sensor on the board, you will cause a short circuit, and that piece of your project will not trigger a sound.
- If you need to remove the board from your project to troubleshoot, just put some fresh paint down in the spots under E0, E11, and GND to reattach to your surface.

LilyPad MP3 Projects

LilyPad MP3 Project 1: Create an Interactive Band T-Shirt!

Music Maker Skills Required

You will need to be able to edit sound files.

Materials

- T-shirt from your favorite band
- Conductive thread
- LilyPad reed switch
- LilyPad MP3 player
- LilyPad LEDs, optional
- MicroSD card on which to put audio files
- Single-cell (3.7-V) LiPo battery

- One thin speaker (between 4 and 8 ohms) or a pair of headphones, two speakers optional
- Soldering iron and solder for attaching speakers to your project (not needed if you use headphones)
- Alligator clips
- Felt or other fabric
- Magnet
- Craft glue

Get started with wearables and interactive textile projects with the LilyPad MP3 player! Soft circuit projects are a great way to bring together many areas of making and skill building in a fun and creative way. This project is a good intermediate project, and I would suggest starting off with a more basic project if you are new to sewing and soft circuits. However, this is something a determined beginner can tackle with planning and patience.

The original LilyPad Arduino was designed for e-textile projects and can be sewn or attached in another way to your wearable project. The LilyPad was created by Dr. Leah Buechley and developed cooperatively with SparkFun Electronics as a wearable piece of technology. It's a great way to get into Arduino projects, and the sketches can be easily tweaked to your project needs. As with the LilyPad MP3 player, the basic LilyPad can be powered by a LiPo battery, has numbered triggers, and can be loaded with new Arduino sketches. For e-textile projects, the LilyPad is a great option because it is washable, and the battery can be recharged via a microUSB cable. The LilyPad MP3 player is a great option for sound projects, especially for those new to Arduino, because you don't have to write and load Arduino sketches for it to play music.

It is very important to plan your circuits before you start sewing your project. A good place to start is with the LilyPad MP3 player itself. First, we'll take a look at the LilyPad so that we can familiarize ourselves with the various parts of the pad that will be necessary for our project (Figure 6.8).

FIGURE 6.8 The LilyPad MP3 can add a musical element to your e-textiles projects!

Starting in the upper-left corner of the LilyPad in the figure, you will see the JST LiPo battery connector. This is where you will plug in your LiPo battery to power your project. Moving clockwise around the LilyPad, the next thing you will see is the headphone jack. As with other devices that play audio, the speaker connection is disabled when you have headphones plugged into the jack. Next, we come to the 5-V FTDI header. This is where you can plug in a FTDI Basic Breakout Board that allows you to plug in a USB cord and recharge your battery or reprogram the LilyPad. Our last stop is the microUSB slot. This is where you will insert the microSD card with the audio files you wish to play.

Now that we are familiar with the inputs where we can plug in items to make our board work, there are more things that you need to know before getting started. In the space on the board below the battery connector and above the microSD card slot, you'll see a power switch that you will use to power your board on and off. Above that switch, you'll see a red light come on under the word "Power." The red light means that your board is "on." To the right, you will see the word "Charge." A yellow light will come on when the battery is being charged or it will sometimes come on if no battery is connected. The light will go off when the battery is fully charged.

Next, we will move on to the 12 pins that you will use to connect the speakers or conductive thread. There are five trigger pins, four speaker pins (two for the right speaker and two for the left speaker), one 3.3-V in/out, one 3.5-V in/out, and a ground. For our project, we will only need to be concerned with trigger, ground, and speaker pins.

Whenever you are working with a circuits project, whether it be paper circuits or soft circuits, it's best to sketch out your plans before you start sewing, painting, or laying down copper tape. If you start sewing before you have figured out the best way to lay out your circuits within your design, you are liable to find yourself having to start over because you may find out that you will not be able to complete the circuit correctly until it's too late. For LilyPad projects, you can also test your circuits before committing your project to fabric. You can connect the alligator clips to your switch or triggers to test that your project is going to work correctly before you start as well.

Now that we have covered the basics of the LilyPad MP3 and soft circuits, we are ready to start planning our project.

Step One

You want to start with planning out your project on paper before you do anything else. One of the best ways to do this is to draw a sketch using paper and pencils. Start by drawing a t-shirt shape, and approximate the design so that you can figure out how you would like to lay out your circuit. This will help you to figure out where to sew your connections, making sure that you do not cross connections, shorting out your project. For this project, you will want to figure out where you will place your LilyPad, the speakers, your switch, and lights if you wish to include another element (Figure 6.9).

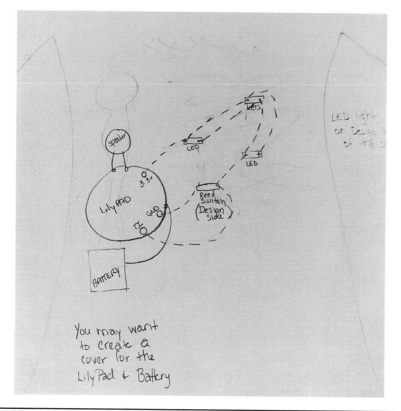

FIGURE 6.9   Draw out your circuit plan before you sew.

Step Two

To test our project before sewing, we will need the sound we wish to use. For this project, we will use our sound editing skills to create a small clip of a song that will play when you push the reed switch. For an easy and free way to get a short sound clip for a project such as this, you may wish to use a free web-based editor such as Audio Trimmer (www.audiotrimmer.com).

Trimming an Audio File with Audio Trimmer for LilyPad MP3

Step One
Upload your sound file.

Step Two
Listen to your file to determine the part you wish to use for your project.

Step Three

Use the green tabs with your mouse or your keyboard's arrow keys to move the tabs to the beginning and end points of the clip you wish to use. Alternately, you can type in the time stamp.

Step Four

Choose whether or not you want to have the sound fade in and/or fade out.

Step Five

Make sure to select MP3 as the output format and then click Download.

Step Six

For use in your project, rename the file by placing the number of the trigger you wish to use on your LilyPad MP3. For example, if you are using trigger 1, your file name should be something like "1 Song Title.mp3."

Step Seven

Load your renamed file onto the microSD card. If you are using audio software, you should load your purchased copy of the song into your audio editing software so that you can take a piece of the song to be triggered by your switch. You need to save your audio file with a specific name so that it will work with your LilyPad MP3. While the player can play a variety of file types, including MP3, WAV, WMI, MID, and so on, you can't call your file something like "Song Title edit" and have it work on your player. As in the preceding example, the file needs to have the trigger number you will be using in your project as the first "word" in the file name. Save your file as "1 Song Title.mp3" or whatever compatible file type you prefer.

The LilyPad MP3 uses Arduino conventions and comes preinstalled with a trigger sketch or program that will cause an audio file to play when any one of the five trigger inputs are grounded. The fact that it comes preprogrammed with this sketch makes it great for beginners because you can get started right away without having to learn how to program using the Arduino software. Once your song file is loaded onto your microSD card, you can test your project to be sure that the file works (Figure 6.10).

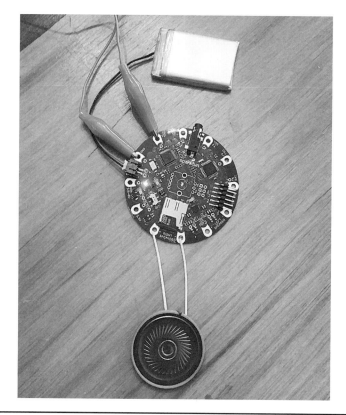

FIGURE 6.10   Use alligator clips to test your clip.

Another great thing about working with the LilyPad is that you don't have to sew your project together until you are sure that everything is working. It is highly recommended that you test your project as you go along because you don't want to get everything sewed onto your shirt and find that something doesn't work. To test your sound file, place the microSD card into the slot on your LilyPad. Next, either plug in a pair of headphones or connect your speaker to the board. Now you can connect an alligator clip to the GND that is located next to the place where you plug in the battery. Turn on your LilyPad, and attach the other end of the alligator clip to T1 or whatever trigger corresponds to your sound file. You should hear the clip play.

Now that you know your audio file works, you can solder your speakers to your LilyPad if you wish to do so. You can attach left and right speakers or just one speaker depending on how comfortable you think having two speakers inside your shirt will be. If you do this project in a different way, two speakers might be optimal. You can use headphones to listen to the sound when triggered, but for more impact, you will want to add a speaker. You also may wish to test your sound with the reed switch. To do this, attach one end of an alligator clip to GND and the other end to the reed switch. Next, attach another alligator clip to T1 and the other end to the reed switch. Touch a magnet to the reed switch, and your sound file should trigger.

Now that you have loaded your audio files, tested your circuits, and attached your speaker(s) to the LilyPad, you are ready to start assembling your project. At this point, you will need the diagram that you created earlier in the project to plan out your circuits. It's crucial that everything is attached correctly in order for your project to work (Figure 6.11).

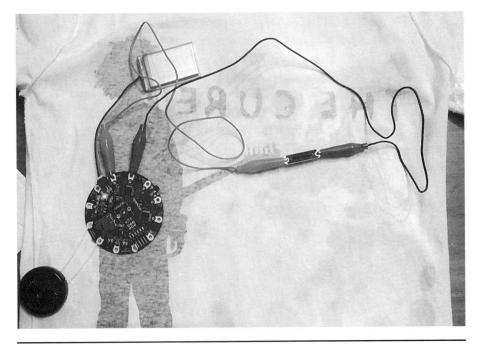

FIGURE 6.11   You can place your project parts on the t-shirt to figure out the best placement of the speaker and battery.

You need to figure out whether you want to sew everything on the outside of your shirt or sew some of the components on the inside. Sewing everything on the outside is easier for those new to hand sewing. Sewing on a t-shirt can be tricky, and you may also wish to use an embroidery hoop to help keep your fabric taut and your stitches tight. For my sample project, I put the speaker, LilyPad MP3, and battery on the inside of my shirt, whereas I stitched the LilyPad LEDs and reed switch on the outside.

Sewing Your Components to Your Project

Step One
Use a small amount of tacky glue to hold your speaker and LilyPad in place.

Step Two
Sew your battery in place using regular thread We will create a battery holder as one of the last steps in the project.

Step Three
Use regular thread to attach your LilyPad MP3 to your shirt using an open terminal to help keep it in place. I used T4 and then across to the (+) left speaker terminal, then I moved up to the speaker and sewed it in place in several places on the wires and the speaker itself (Figure 6.12).

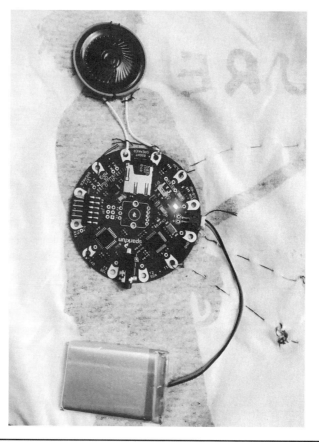

FIGURE 6.12   Use regular thread to attach your speaker and battery pack.

Step Four

Now that your major pieces are in place, you are ready to sew your circuits. From terminal 1 (T1 or whatever terminal your sound is on), use the conductive thread to sew a straight stitch to one side of your reed switch. Tie off your stitch.

NOTE: To sew a straight stitch, you will come up with your needle from the bottom of the fabric at *A*; a short distance from *A* you will put the needle back through the fabric at *B*. Make sure that your stitches are tight. If they are too long or too loose, you may find that your connection is not good, and your sound or lights will just flicker on and off (Figures 6.13 through 6.15).

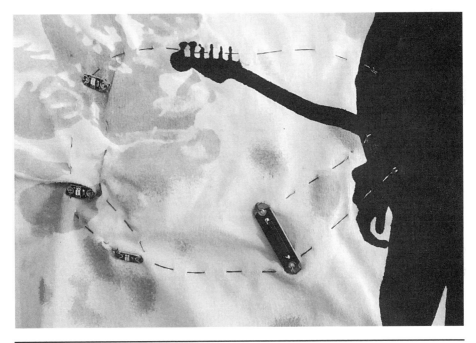

FIGURE 6.13   Sew your LEDs and switch to the front of your shirt.

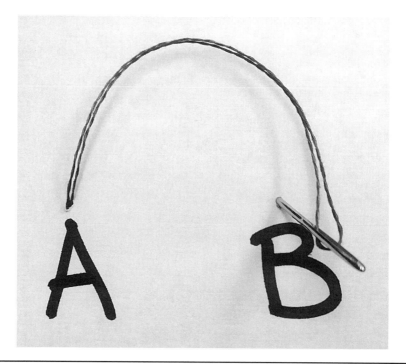

Figure 6.14   Sew a straight stitch by coming up at A and going back down at B.

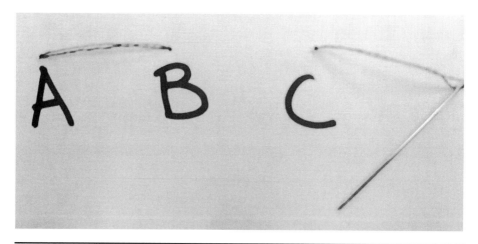

Figure 6.15   Come up again at C and continue to sew like this.

Step Five

Use conductive thread to sew a straight stitch from the ground or GND to the other side of the reed switch. Tie off your stitch (Figure 6.16).

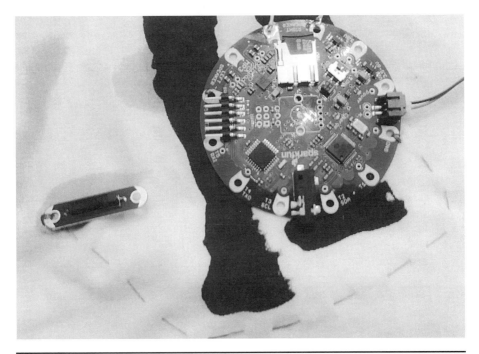

Figure 6.16   Sew from Ground to one side of the Reed Switch.

Step Six

Use conductive thread to sew a straight stitch from the 3.3-V terminal to the (+) positive terminals on your LilyPad LEDs, ending at the side of the reed switch connected to your sound. In my project, this is T1. Tie off your stitch (Figure 6.17).

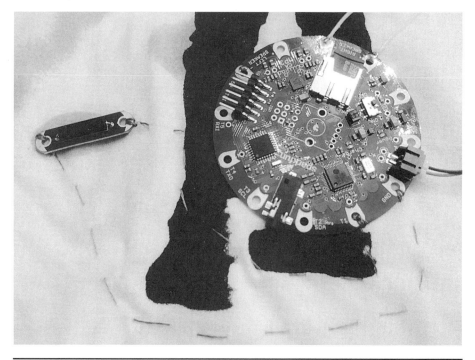

Figure 6.17   Sew from the 3.3-V terminal to connect your lights and sound to the switch.

Step Seven

Use conductive thread to sew a straight stitch from the (–) negative terminal of your first LilyPad LED to the negative terminals on your remaining LEDs and ending at the grounded side of the reed switch. Tie off your stitch.

Step Eight

Use a piece of felt or other fabric to create a battery holder for your project. Cut the piece of felt or fabric into a shape that will hold and cover your battery. Once you have the piece cut out, sew it in place on your shirt so that the battery sits neatly inside on the bottom of the "pocket" (Figure 6.18).

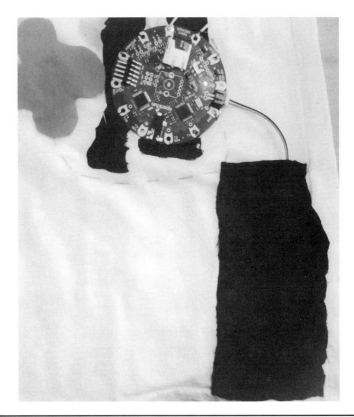

Figure 6.18   Create a battery holder or cover for your components inside the shirt.

Step Nine

Create a magnetic switch to turn on your project. Cut a shape that matches your t-shirt's design out of a small piece of felt. Using tacky glue, glue your magnet to this shape. Sew the shape onto your t-shirt so that you can then put it over the reed switch to turn it on and have your shirt come to life (Figure 6.19)!

FIGURE 6.19   Show off your shirt and amaze your friends!

Your project is now complete and ready to show off to your friends and family!

LilyPad MP3 Project 2: Interactive Sound Pillows

Now that we have tried a project using one terminal for sound and adding lights, we can try a project using more than one sound. You will incorporate recording skills as well as sewing skills in this fun and easy e-textile project.

As we did in the preceding project, we want to plan what we want to do before we start sewing or recording. Will your pillow be using sounds you create, song clips, words, or what?

Materials

- Felt in various colors
- Poly fill
- Conductive thread
- Regular thread or embroidery floss
- LilyPad MP3 player
- Snap assortment, reed switches, or design your own switch
- Magnets if using reed switches
- MicroSD card
- Speaker(s)
- Single-cell (3.7-V) LiPo battery
- Craft glue
- Alligator clips
- Recording equipment (iPad, cellphone, microphone and computer, or however you prefer to record sound)

Once you have decided on the theme for your project, record yourself saying the words or making the sounds that you will use in your project. You can record each word or sound individually, or you can record them all on one track. If you record on one track, you can use the audio trimmer in the first LilyPad project to clip each word you wish to use in your project. Remember that there are five terminals from which you can have sounds trigger on the LilyPad MP3 player. Once you have your words or sounds ready, be sure to name each file using the number scheme that we used in the first project. For example, the sound that will trigger from Terminal 1 can be named "1 Sound.mp3" followed by "2 Sound.mp3," and so on. Copy your sound files to your microSD card, and insert the card into your LilyPad MP3 player.

Now that you have your sound ready and loaded onto the microSD card, you can begin laying out your project. The best way to plan your project is to start with paper and pencil and sketch out your design ideas. It is always a good idea to have a diagram to work from so that you don't end up with a design that doesn't work when you start sewing. For this project, a fun added activity would be to design your own switch for the sounds or experiment using different items such as snaps to create the switch. You can also use a reed switch, as we did in the shirt project (Figure 6.20).

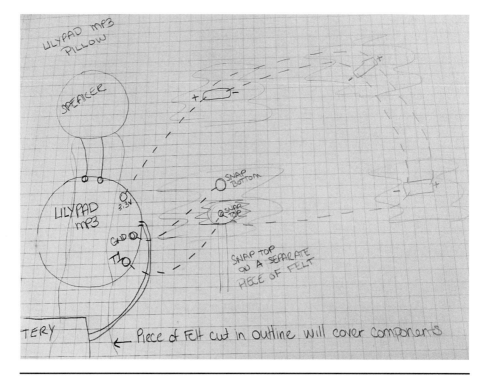

Figure 6.20   Sketch out your design first.

For this project, you will have switches for each sound, so you will want to plan not only where you want each piece of the design to be but also the best way to set up each switch. Each switch will be connected to the ground, which you can connect either individually or run one stitch from the ground to each switch. In turn, each of your five triggers will be connected to the other side of the switch. You can test your switches using alligator clips, as we did in the preceding project to be sure that your sound will trigger (Figure 6.21).

Once you know that your sounds are working and you have your project sketched out, you are ready to sew. First, you will want to attach your speaker(s), battery, and LilyPad to your felt. You can use a small amount of felt or tacky glue to keep the pieces in place until you have sewn all your connections to your pillow. You can incorporate a cover for these components as part of your design, making sure that you will still be able to access the switch to turn the LilyPad on and charge your battery.

As you work on attaching each part of your project, you will want to test to be sure the connections are working so that you don't get everything sewn together and then discover that there is a problem with one of the sounds.

Figure 6.21 Remember to test your sound or sounds before sewing.

Once you have all your components attached, you are ready to add any finishing touches. You can use felt glue or regular thread to sew on embellishments. Another option would be to add lights by creating a simple circuit using a switched LilyPad battery holder and a few LilyPad LEDs or even add a LilyTiny for effects. You can add the lights in series by sewing the (+) positive terminal of the battery holder to the positive terminal in each of the LEDs and repeat on the side with the (–) negative terminal. Just remember, if you are going to add more conductive elements, you want to sketch out your plan so that you don't short out any of your circuits. The conductive thread cannot overlap or touch the ends of the thread from the other parts of your project or you can create a short circuit.

Sound and Recording Projects

Podcasting

Podcasting is a great long-term project that can combine audio recording and editing techniques along with writing, art, and even getting into business skills. This is a great project for really bringing together those twenty-first-century skills that will be part of a successful future for today's young people. Podcasting can be an individual project, but it also makes a great group project. It will give participants an opportunity to explore different aspects of bringing a podcast to life that will help them on the path to discovering what they like to do.

While adults may be familiar with podcasts such as Serial, Nerdist, Five Thirty Eight, and others, younger people may not be as familiar with this medium. A great way to get started with this project is to explore podcasts that are already out there. Podcasts cover such a wide range of interests that it should be easy to find at least one that speaks to your own or your group's interests. Here are some good podcasts to start off with if you would rather start here, or you can explore the variety of podcasts available through your favorite music service such as Google Play Music, iTunes, or Spotify. Please note that not all podcasts are for young audiences, and you will see some marked "Explicit—Some content not suitable for children." If you are working with a young class, you may wish to preselect the podcasts you use with your group.

Good Podcasts for Kids and Families
- The Radio Adventures of Eleanor Amplified (WHYY)
- The Alien Adventures of Finn Caspian: Science Fiction for Kids (Typedrawer Media)
- The Radio Adventures of Dr. Floyd Official Podcast (Grant Baciocco & Doug Price, DoctorFloyd.com/Saturday Morning Media)
- Tumble Science Podcast for Kids (Tumble Media/Wondry)

Good Podcasts for Makers, Gamers, and Nerds
- Making It with Jimmy Diresta, Bob Clagett, and David Picciuto
- Nintendo Voice Chat
- The Weekly Planet
- Batman News
- MakingStarWars.net's Now, This Is Podcasting

Good Podcasts for Music Lovers
- Song Exploder
- Monstercat Podcast
- EDM Producer Podcast
- AudioSkills Podcast
- Note to Scene

This is by no means an exhaustive list of podcasts, but it is a great place to start exploring different kinds of podcasts and the different approaches to creating a podcast. Some of these podcasts are short four- or five-minute serial-style stories in the tradition of old radio stories; others are more in the moment, focusing on current topics; and some are selections of music featured on a weekly basis. As you can see, there is no one way to approach podcasting.

By exploring podcasts though Google Play, iTunes, or Spotify, you can also get an idea of what the finished product looks like and start to think about the elements of a good podcast. If you are working on podcasting as part of a series of programs or classes, you can have students take some time exploring selected podcasts and brainstorming what these podcasts have in common and what they think goes into a good podcast.

Part One: Getting Started

The first thing you will want to decide before anything else is what your podcast is going to be about. You have now had the chance to check out a variety of podcasts and can see that they can be on any topic and even include dramatic productions. If you will be tackling podcasting as part of a class, you will want the participants to form teams and have the teams figure out what they would like to work on.

Now that you have figured out what your podcast is going to be about, you are ready to tackle the various elements that go into a complete podcast. There is no particular order in which you need to work, so a good place to start is to talk about all the tasks that you will need to complete to create your podcast.
These include

- *Podcast title.* As you can see in the preceding examples, all podcasts have a title that makes it easy to find in the vast libraries of available podcasts.
- *Logo.* One element you will notice when browsing podcast listings is that each one has a distinct logo that often includes the name of the podcast.

- *Script or outline of the episode.* You need to plan what you want to talk about in each episode. If you are doing a dramatic series, you will definitely want a script so that each player knows his or her lines.
- *Music.* You may wish to have a theme song for your podcast.

If you are working on podcasting in a group setting, you should have the students either divide themselves up into teams or you divide them up based on their interests. You can also do podcasting in a group without the need to divide up into smaller groups. Now that you have everyone paired up to work, each group should begin working on brainstorming ideas for their podcast. At this time, there's no need to be selective; have the students write down their ideas so that they have a selection of topics from which to choose. Give the group about 10 to 15 minutes for brainstorming. During this time, you can move around the room making sure that the groups are focused and helping them along by asking questions guide their brainstorming.

Once this brainstorming session is up, you can regroup and have each group share some of the ideas they came up with. Sharing the ideas can help others who may be struggling to come up with their own ideas by having a look at what others have come up with. You can stretch this part of the activity by discussing their ideas and topics and how they think they would work in a format that relies solely on listening without the help of visual clues. Now that they have some ideas about what they would like to talk about, you can move into developing logos and titles for the podcasts.

There are several different ways you can approach coming up with a title and a logo in a group setting. You can have each team brainstorm its own ideas or the class can brainstorm as a group. Again, give the teams about 10 minutes or so to brainstorm title ideas. Once this time is up, the groups can work to finalize their titles. They can vote on their favorite or create a mash-up title combining the ideas of the individuals in the group. Combining ideas can be a great way to include everyone's input and give ownership of the project to the whole group.

Now that the groups have selected their titles, they are ready to get started on the logo. Again, there is no right way to do this. The groups can brainstorm what they would like their logos to look like, each individual can create his or her own design, or perhaps there is an aspiring artist in the group who would like to design the logo. The logo design process is also an opportunity to introduce the students to digital design tools such as the online graphic design tool Canva or iPad apps such as Adobe Sketch or Illustrator. The groups should come up with their own approach in logo design because this should be a process by which kids can work with various aspects of the project to find what they are interested in (Figure 6.22).

Figure 6.22   Design a logo for your podcast.

Part Two

Now that your group is familiar with podcasting and has its ideas together, group members are ready to start working on their first podcast. Before getting started with recording the podcast, your teams will need to put their ideas on paper so that they aren't recording without having a handle on what they want to say or the flow of their program. Depending on the type of podcast, you'll want to have an outline of the conversation or a script in hand before you start recording. In my experience, a lot of kids are shy to talk on a microphone, so having a script or outline is essential before they start the recording process. A script will also help each speaker know his or her role so that you don't have everyone talking over one another. If your group wants to keep the podcast more conversational, they will want to at least put together an outline of what they are going to talk about. There is nothing worse than getting in front of a microphone and having a lot of ums and ahs as part of the recording.

Sample Podcast Outline
- Soundz from the Garage—A Podcast about Making and Music
- Introduction
- Theme music plays (either self-composed or music from Creative Commons)

- First topic—Music news or discuss a recent favorite track or album. For example, "This week we're going to talk about upcoming shows that we are excited to see."
- Second topic—Maker news of the week, where we discuss something interesting in the maker community or a maker tool that we tried. Example, "This week we'll explore the Bare Conductive Touch Board. This board is a great maker tool for musicians."
- Third topic—Discuss something related to music technology or creating music. Example, "This week we're going to talk about the littleBits Synth Kit and some ideas we have about music bits we'd like to see."
- Fourth topic—Discuss projects we are working on or planning. Example, "This week we're exploring a little bit about how we can use the LilyPad MP3 player to create improved band t-shirts."
- Closing thoughts

As you can see, you don't have to have your entire show scripted out, but you may want to fill in more details about the specific things you want to talk about. For a more conversational podcast, however, you don't need to script out the entire show because you want it to sound more natural. Here teams will create a script or outline for their podcast. For an extended session, you will want to have the teams begin working with the microphone because they will need some practice before they feel comfortable with recording their voices.

For the collaborative aspect of this project and to encourage the sharing of ideas when the group is not together, you may want to explore using a collaboration site or app to help keep the ideas flowing. Trello and Slack can be used on a PC or Mac and have apps available as well. In Trello, you can create boards where ideas can be shared. Slack uses channels to bring together ideas in one place, allowing for sharing and commenting. If your participants wish to continue their podcast after the project period, using one of these collaborative tools is a great way to keep the ideas going.

Part Three

Now that everyone has their ideas in place, it's time to start recording the podcasts. There are several approaches you can take to recording depending on what equipment you have available to you and whether you wish to invest in some items for better sound quality in your recordings.

Equipment

- iPad with GarageBand
- Desktop or laptop computer with Audacity, Ableton, or other sound recording software
- For recording with a microphone, mixer, such as the Behringer five-channel mixer (about $60 from Amazon)
- Lightning-to-USB adapter if using iPad
- Microphone of your choice
- For recording through the headphone jack of an iPad, compact microphone designed for use with iPads such as the iRig Mic Cast compact vocal mic (about $40 from Amazon)

If you have a PC or laptop, you can record into a freeware program such as Audacity. When I ran this program as part of the Minecraft in Real Life Club at the Middletown Free Library, the kids spent some time working with all three setups in order to compare how they worked and to get comfortable working with the recording aspect as well as with GarageBand and Audacity. This exercise provides an opportunity for participants to explore various methods of recording, which is great for adaptability and finding the method that they prefer for this kind of recording project.

Here you will have the teams explore recording with the tools you have available. The goal should be for all groups to complete a short 5- to 15-minute podcast. I have learned through conducting these kinds of programs that goal setting is important to keep the teams on track and so that something is accomplished in the time you have together.

If some members of the group are more interested in music creation than speaking, you can have the groups split up and work according to interest. One team may be focused on scripting and recording the podcast, while the other team may wish to work on recording theme music and putting together any sound effects they wish to use in the podcast.

Part Four

Now that the groups have recorded their first short podcast, you will want to start the editing process. The first thing the groups may wish to do is take a listen to their recording. Sometimes we think something is perfect when we first finish it, but when you go back and take a second look, it's not as great as you first thought. The groups will want to be sure that they are happy with what they have recorded and start asking themselves questions about what they have captured.

- How is the sound quality? Are some speakers too loud, too soft? Is everyone easy to understand?
- Are there long gaps in time where no one is speaking, or is everyone speaking over one another?
- How is the content of the podcast? Is it on topic, or is time spent talking about topics not related to the stated content of the recording?

These questions will help the teams to identify what they need to fix in the editing process and to decide whether there are things they need to rerecord.

In the editing process, you can add in the theme music and any other sounds you want to add to enhance the production. This stage of the project will really bring in some of the knowledge that you have learned from earlier projects in this book, especially if you worked with the littleBits Synth Kit learning how the envelope, filter, and so on work. In the editing process, not only will you be adding music and sound effects and making sure that your content is good, but you will also be checking on the quality of the audio you recorded. Is it too loud or too quiet? Can it be fixed in the editing process, or do you have to rerecord it?

In this part, you want to spend your time editing and perfecting your podcasts to get them ready for publication. Once each group has given its podcast a second listen, it's time to share all the podcasts with the group for further critique. This is an opportunity to have each podcast evaluated by potential listeners and to give constructive feedback on what was good and what can be improved. The following Podcast Evaluation Checklist will be helpful, and each person or group should have a copy of it in order to take notes and provide feedback. Each podcast should be listened to once through without interruption. At the end of the first listen, go around the room for suggestions and feedback on the podcast the group just listened to. You will want to set some ground rules so that teams can receive feedback without hurt feelings. Once you have completed this listening session, each group should go back and discuss the feedback they received and decide if they wish to make further edits.

Editing can be a long process, so you may wish to use more than one session to have the groups work on editing their podcasts. Groups will want to have a publication-ready podcast by the Final Part, where they will learn about publishing their podcasts and actually publish their first episode.

Final Part

In this Final Part, everyone will learn how to publish their podcast. This is pretty exciting because participants will be able to share their work with family and

Podcasting Evaluation Checklist

What to Listen For	Good/Yes	Bad/No	Notes
Sound quality (too loud, soft, sound levels consistent)			
Flow of the story or conversation			
Is the content on topic?			
Does the story make sense?			
If there are sound effects, are they timed correctly?			
Are the sound effects or music appropriate?			
Anything else you notice or think should be changed or added			

friends. If you are an educator or librarian, this is a great way to promote your program and get support for future audio programs in your space.

How to Publish Your Podcast with SoundCloud and iTunes

First, you will need to create an account with SoundCloud (http://soundcloud .com) if you don't already have one. Once you have your account, you are ready to upload your finished podcast and set up your account so that your podcast can be shared on iTunes and other podcasting distributors.

In order to share your podcast to iTunes, you will need to have the following things completed in your SoundCloud account:

- One episode of your podcast uploaded on your account
- Your podcast's logo artwork as your profile picture (artwork should be between 1,400 × 1,400 and 3,000 × 3,000 pixels)
- A description of your podcast in the bio section of your profile
- Updated content settings to create an RSS feed

Once you have your account set up, you are ready to upload your first episode!

If you are using an iPad, it is very easy to upload your recording to SoundCloud (Figure 6.23).

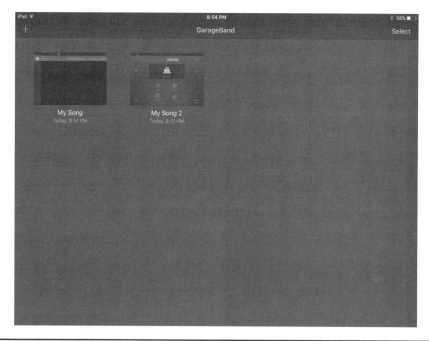

Figure 6.23   On an iPad, choose your file in GarageBand.

On the screen where you saved your audio files in GarageBand, hold your finger down on the track what you want to upload. You will then see three icons appear in the upper left-hand corner of the screen (Figure 6.24).

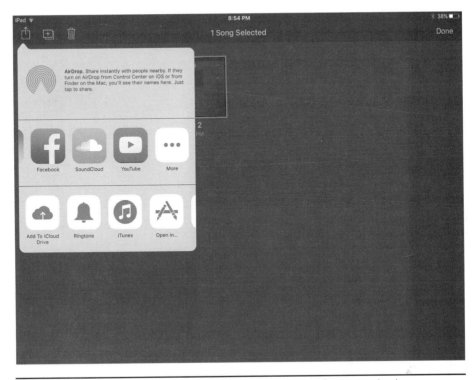

Figure 6.24 Choose SoundCloud to open the options screen for your upload.

Click on the icon that looks like a box with an arrow pointing up. This will open up the choices for sharing your creation. Scroll the icons in the tray to the left until you see SoundCloud; then tap on it. If you are not already logged in, you will be asked to log in to your account. Once you are logged in, you can change the export options, such as changing the name of the track, adding a photo, adjusting sound quality, and so on (Figure 6.25).

Once you have made all your selections, click on Share in the upper right-hand corner of the box, and your file will be posted to your SoundCloud account. Once your file is on SoundCloud, it will be available to others. If you are looking for a wider audience for your show, having your podcast already loaded on SoundCloud, as you did earlier, you can easily publish to iTunes and Google Play Music.

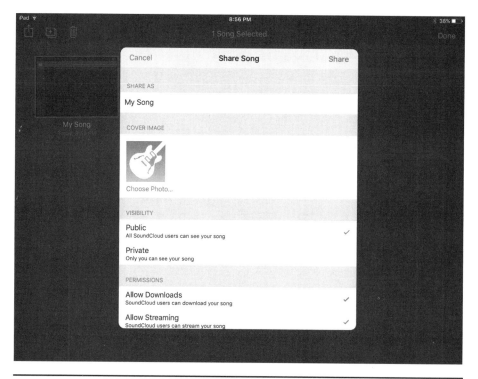

FIGURE 6.25   Enter as much information as you would like about your recording.

micro:bit Project

The micro:bit is a small programmable computer created by the BBC in collaboration with 29 partners to provide a fun and easy entry to learning computer coding skills. The micro:bit is given to every child as he or she enters year seven of school because the United Kingdom is facing a shortage of skills in the technology fields, similar to what is being seen in the United States. The goal of this project is to provide kids with the opportunity to learn the science, computing, and engineering skills that are needed in today's workforce.

The micro:bit has a lot of potential for a variety of projects because there is so much packed into this tiny little board. This tiny computer is powered by a 16-MHz ARM Cortex-M0 microcontroller with 256 kB of Flash and 16 kB of RAM.

Getting to Know Your micro:bit

- *Light array.* A 5 × 5 grid on which you can display images or text that you design or an existing design you can choose when coding your project. The light array also functions as a light sensor.
- *Buttons.* "A" button is on the right and "B" button is on the left. These are great for creating a game or triggering a sound.
- *Edge pins.* These can be used to hook up external components using alligator clips (Figures 6.26 and 6.27).
- *USB port.* Use this port to plug your microUSB cable into a computer to power the micro:bit and upload the code for your project.
- *Reset button.* Use this button to reset your micro:bit and start your new code.

FIGURE **6.26**   This is the front of your micro:bit.

Figure 6.27   This is the back of your micro:bit.

- *JST battery connector.* Connect an external battery pack to your micro:bit so that your projects don't need to be tethered to your computer or tablet.
- *Bluetooth/antenna.* Communicate with your tablet or phone using Bluetooth, or you can use the radio antenna to communicate between two micro:bits.
- *Accelerometer/compass.* The onboard accelerometer can measure gravitational force, whereas the compass can detect orientation of the board.
- *Microcontroller/temperature sensor.* Yes, the microcontroller also functions a temperature sensor.

There are several different coding editors that you can use to start coding your first project. These coding editors are both block-based programming editors as well as text-based editors that will help you to learn JavaScript and Python programming languages.

Basic LED Art and Sound Project

For this project, we'll design small 5- × 5-pixel art graphics to be displayed and choose a sound to be played when we touch an object that conducts a small amount of electricity.

Materials

- One mirco:bit board
- Alligator clips
- MicroUSB cable
- Battery pack
- Conductive objects such as aluminum foil, conductive fabric, Play-doh
- Graph paper or plain white paper. Create some 5 × 5 designs on your graph paper before you get started coding.

To get started, go to https://makecode.microbit.org/ to access the micro:bit JavaScript code editor we will be using for our project. When you open the editor to create a new project, you will see a workspace that consists of three areas. On the left, you'll see a picture of a micro:bit. This is where you can test your code to see if it works. In the center, you will see the list of codes you can choose from to build your project. On the right is where you will build the code for your project (Figure 6.28).

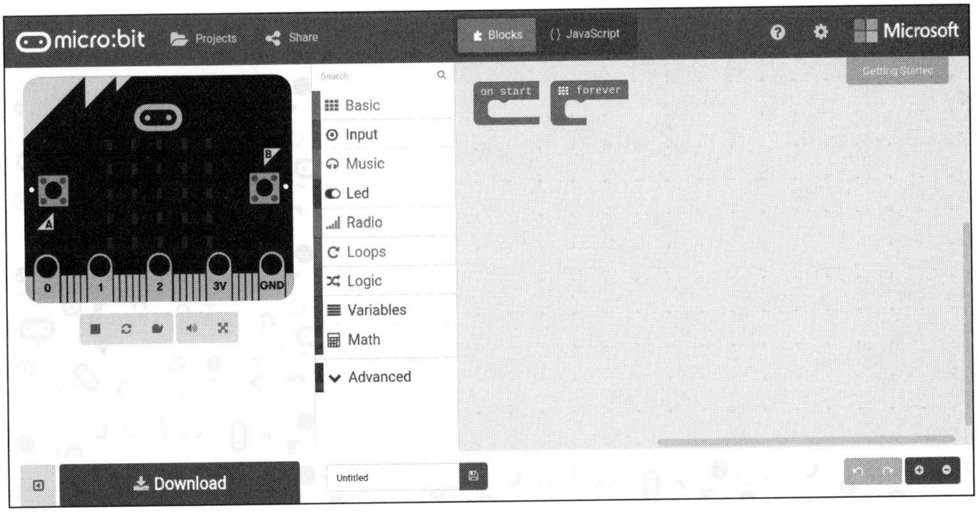

Figure 6.28   Open a new project to get started programming your micro:bit.

For this introductory project, you'll be using code blocks from BASIC, INPUT, and MUSIC.

Step One

Move the "On Start" and "Forever" command blocks to the Trash by dragging them to the middle panel. You will see a Trash Can icon appear when you do this. Place both items in the Trash.

Step Two

Click on INPUT in the middle of the screen, and choose the command block `on pin0 pressed`, and move it to your workspace. Change `pin0` to `pin1`.

Step Three

Click on MUSIC in the code column, and choose the command you wish to work with. I chose "Start Melody Dadadum Repeating Once" for my project. You can also choose "Play Tone Middle C for 1 Beat" or any combination you wish. You could create a melody yourself or use one of the preprogrammed melodies.

Example Melody

- Choose "Repeat 4 Times" from LOOPS if you want your melody to loop. This allows you to play a series of notes several times without having to write or move blocks to repeat the notes.
- Create your melody using "Play Middle C for 1 Beat" from MUSIC. When you click on "Middle C" to change the note, a small keyboard will pop up, and you can choose the note you want to use
- Repeat this second step until you have built your melody.
- Change the number of times to repeat the loop to create your melody (Figure 6.29).

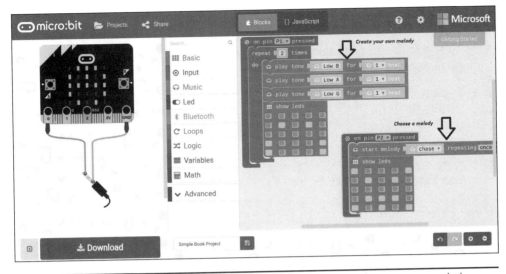

FIGURE 6.29   You can add a musical element to your program by creating your own melody or using a pre-recorded option.

Step Four

Choose "Show LEDs" from BASIC. You can now use the designs you already plotted out on your graph paper to create the picture that will be created by the LEDs on your micro:bit when the pin is triggered. Click on the boxes in the LED command in your workspace that correspond to the ones you plotted on your graph paper to create your image.

Step Five

Now that you have created your LED images, you can connect the "Show LEDs" block to each of the melodies for each of the pins. You can test your project to see how it will work by clicking on the pin on the image of the micro:bit on the left-hand side of your screen.

Step Six

Save your project. At the bottom of the screen under the command code blocks, you will see a small picture of a floppy disc and space to input the name of your project. Name your project, and click on the disc to save it. When you click on the Save button, the file will also download to your computer.

Step Seven

Download your project to your micro:bit. First, you will need to connect your micro:bit to your computer. When you connect it, you'll see the orange light flash on the back of the bit, and you'll see its files on your computer. Now open the file where your downloaded files were saved, and drag the project file to the micro:bit to send the file to the bit. The yellow light on the back of the micro:bit will flash while the program is installed. Once the file is copied to the micro:bit, eject it from your computer and disconnect it.

Step Eight: Setting Up Your Project

Connect the battery pack to your micro:bit. If yours didn't come with a battery pack, keep it connected to your computer to power it. Hook up your speaker by connecting an alligator clip to pin 0 and another alligator clip to GND (ground). Connect the other end of each alligator clip to copper wire at each end of the speaker cable (Figure 6.30).

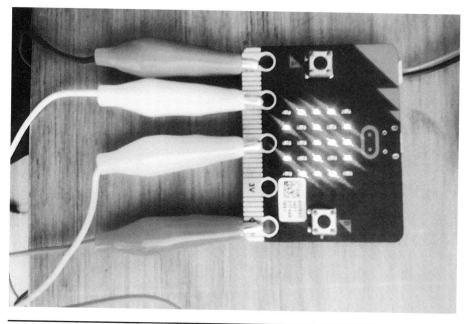

Figure 6.30   Hook up your micro:bit using alligator clips.

Step Nine: Setting Up Your Triggers

Now you want to figure out how to trigger your program. Connect an alligator clip to pin 1 and pin 2. You will then connect the other end of your alligator clip to whatever you will touch to play the sound and picture on your micro:bit. You can use any kind of conductive material such as aluminum foil, conductive fabric, Play-doh, and so on. Connect another alligator clip to GND. Hold the ground wire in your fingers and then touch the item that will trigger the sound. You will then see your creation come to life (Figure 6.31)!

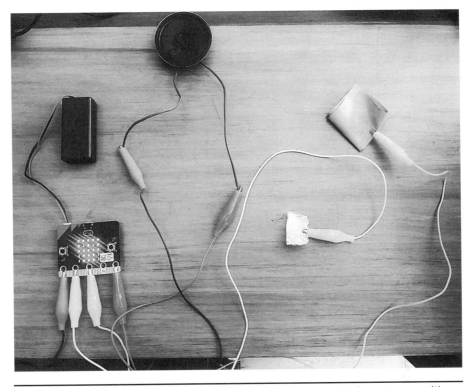

FIGURE 6.31   As with the Makey Makey, you can set up a variety of triggers to use with your project.

NOTE: You can also see what the typed-out code would look like by clicking on JavaScript at the top of the coding page. It's always a good idea to take a look at what your block code looks like in written form because part of what you are learning by using something like the micro:bit is coding. In real life, computer programmers do not use block code but write out the code, so you will want to eventually move from coding in block to coding in text (Figure 6.32).

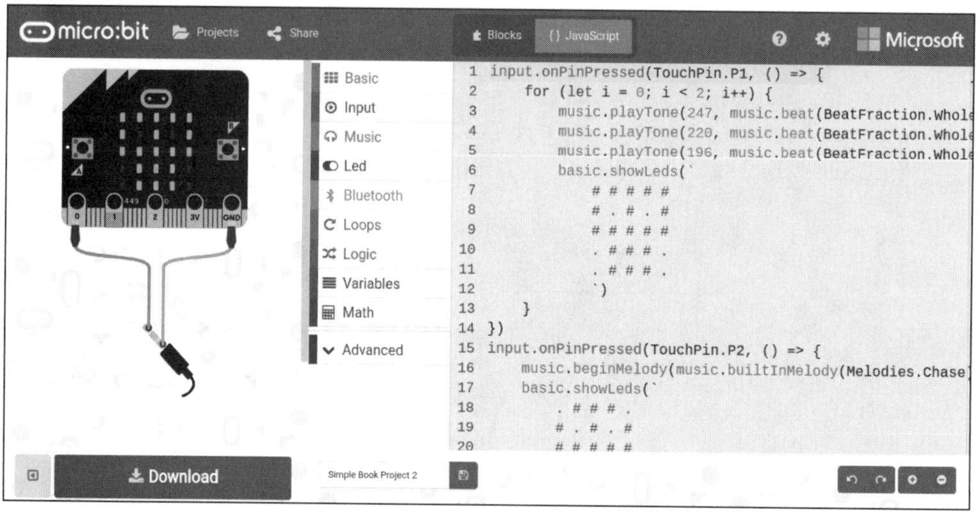

FIGURE 6.32   The JavaScript code.

Storytelling with Sound

This is a fun project that combines some elements from the previous projects. The object is to tell a short story of one to two minutes using only sound. Before you begin putting your story together, think about how sounds and music are used in movies and especially in cartoons to convey meaning. You may wish to watch a few episodes of *SpongeBob* or *Looney Tunes* to really get the idea.

For this project, you can record your own sound effects or select sounds using the many royalty-free sound sites online to gather your effects. A few good sites are mentioned in the Bare Conductive project earlier in this chapter.

To start, you will want to write out a story or a sketch of your idea so that you can start thinking about the kinds of sounds you want to use. Think about the atmosphere you want to create, what kinds of sounds can relay the action taking place, the emotions your characters are feeling, and so on. Is it a love story, a funny story, or a scary story? Once you have these kinds of questions answered, you can start hunting down your sounds or going out into the field to make recordings of the sounds you want to use. There's no need to get fancy with the recording; you can use a recording app on your phone to do this.

Once you have your sounds recorded or you have chosen a selection of sounds to tell your story from the online sound libraries, you are ready to put together your story.

Here are the sound effects I chose from the SoundBible site for my sound story:

- City sidewalk and pedestrian sounds
- Martian scanner
- Mars attacks
- People screaming
- Laser blasts
- Bomb exploding
- Soldiers marching
- Cheering 3

Putting Your Story Together in Audacity

Step One
Open Audacity and create a new file (Figure 6.33).

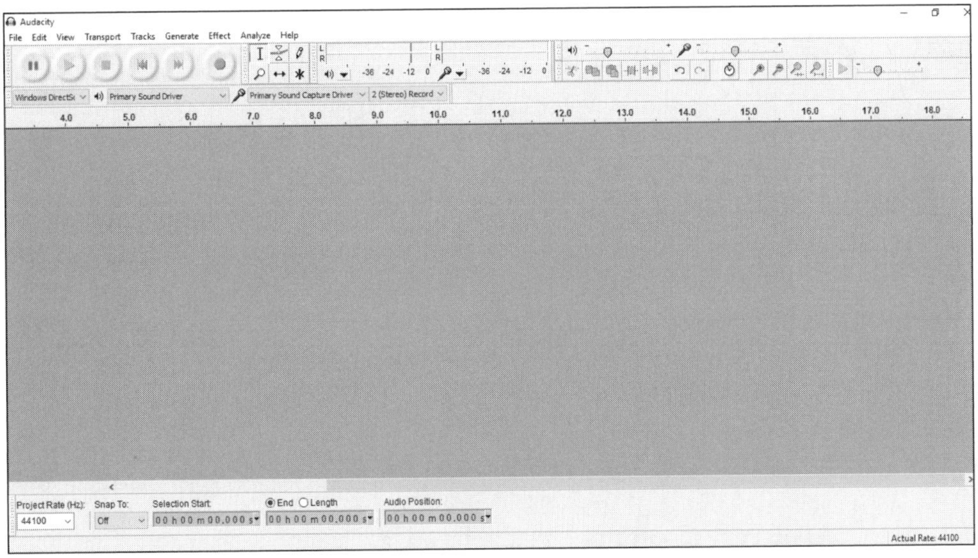

FIGURE **6.33**   Open a new Audacity file.

Step Two
Click on File > Import > Audio Tracks to import the sound files into the program. You will repeat this step to add all your audio tracks for your story (Figure 6.34).

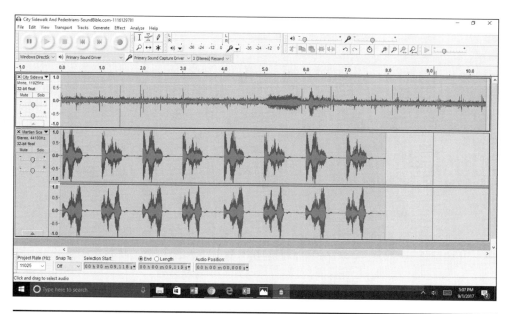

Figure 6.34 Add your audio tracks.

Step Three

Now that your track is in Audacity, you can edit it, such as making the track longer, shorter, and so on. You can make the windows of the tracks you are not working on smaller by clicking on the small arrow at the bottom of the track information on the left-hand side of your screen. This makes it easier to work with one track at a time while still seeing where the other tracks are in your screen. Select the section of the track you wish to edit by using your mouse to highlight it, and then choose your action. I'm going to cut and paste my sound to come in at a later time in the story by clicking on the scissors icon or by clicking on Edit > Cut. Then I will click in the track on which I am working at the place I would like to move it to, and click on the Paste icon or choose Edit > Paste (Figures 6.35 and 6.36).

Step Four

Repeat Steps Two and Three until you have all your files in Audacity and edited to the position you would like them to be to tell your story.

You have now created your story in Audacity. Save your file in the format of your choice. You are now ready to share your story with your classmates, friends, and family. As a fun exercise in a group setting, share each story and have the students write down their interpretation of the story they just heard. Go around the room and have each person share his or her ideas of what the story was about and to see how many were able to accurately interpret your sound story.

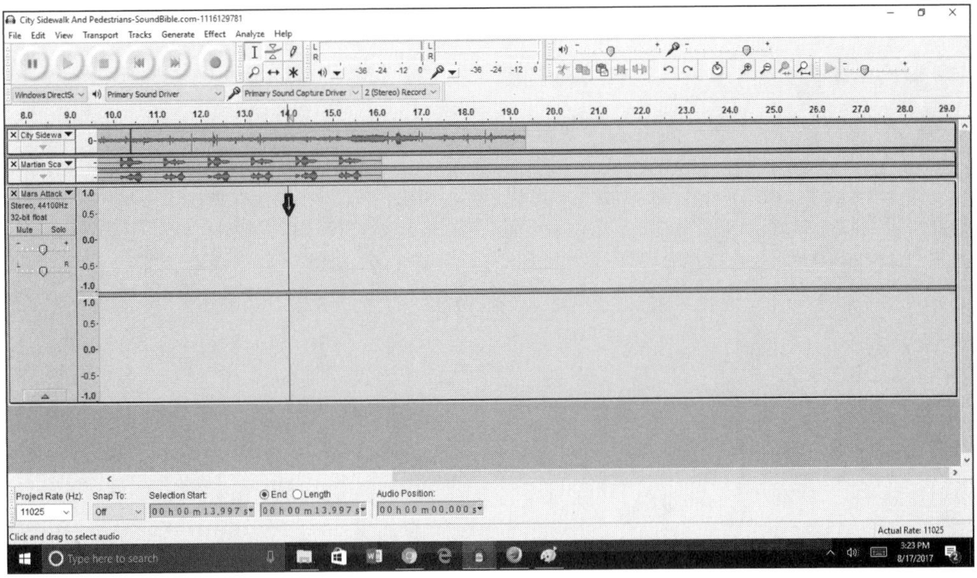

FIGURE **6.35**   Move your track to where you would like it to come in.

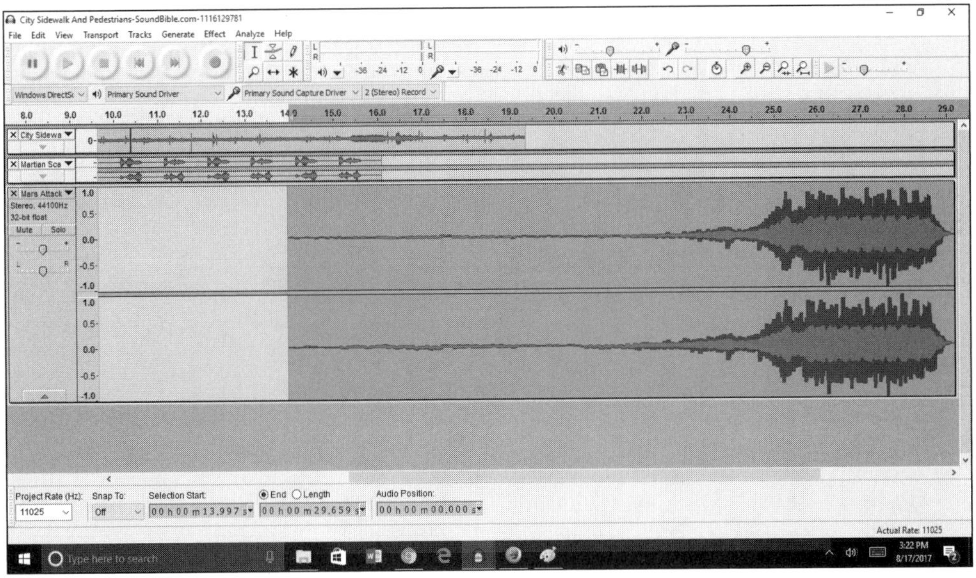

FIGURE **6.36**   Your track is now where you moved it.

CHAPTER 7

Maker Projects for Music Lovers

While most of this book has focused on projects that involve making music and sound, why stop there? There are fun ways to take your love of music and sound to create fun and creative craft projects to decorate your room or your holidays or to take on the go and more!

Exploring 3D Design

3D printers are one of the first things people think about when they hear the word *makerspace*, and many makerspaces in schools, libraries, and the community have a printer that is accessible to the public. Tinkercad is a great entry point to learning how to design in a 3D environment. Many young makers who have experience playing Minecraft find it easy to get started designing in Tinkercad. Another way to explore 3D design is through 3D carving. Machines such as Inventables' Carvey are easy to get started with. Easel is the design software used for creating designs for carving on the Carvey. Easel, like Tinkercad, is a free web-based design tool, so you can explore design and get familiar with these tools even if you don't have access to a machine with which to print or carve.

3D Album Covers

Inventables' 6- × 6-inch tiles are the perfect material to dream up artwork for a favorite album or song. For inspiration, take a look at some classic album artwork throughout the years. You can do a simple Internet search or take a look at some lists that others have put together, such as *Wired Magazine*'s "Best Album Art of All Time" (www.wired.com/2010/06/gallery-album-covers/) or *NME*'s "50 Iconic

Indie Album Covers: The Fascinating Stories Behind the Sleeves" (http://bit.ly/musicsound01). You can also get inspiration by looking through your own or a friend's collection or even visiting your local record shop.

Now that you've been inspired, it's time to get started with our project.

Materials

- Desktop, laptop, or Chromebook
- Easel account
- Access to Carvey (optional; you can still design in Easel without Carvey)
- 6- × 6-inch HDPE two-color tile

Step One

Create an account at Inventables to log in to Easel. To do this, go to www .inventables.com/technologies/easel, and click on Explore Easel. When you get to the login screen, click "I am a new customer," enter your e-mail address and name, and create a password. Click Continue to complete the login process.

Step Two

There are a few changes you need to make to the settings before you get started with your design. It's always a good idea to set up your workspace first so that you can use the preview pane to see how your design will carve (Figure 7.1).

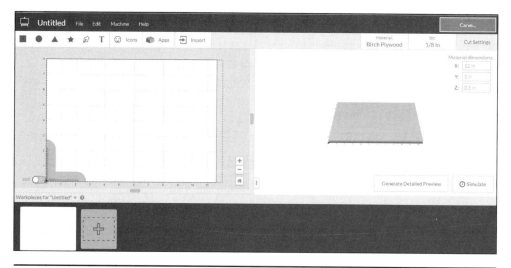

Figure 7.1   Let's set up our workspace before we start designing.

Step Three

Click on Machine, and choose Carvey (Figure 7.2).

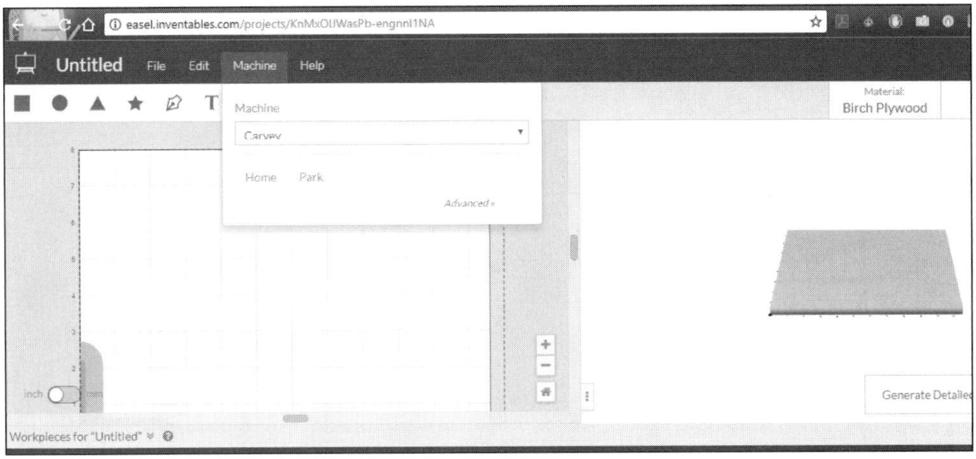

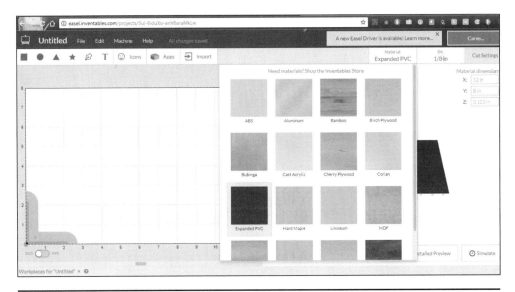

FIGURE 7.2   Select Carvey or the machine you will be carving with from the pull-down menu.

Step Four

Click on Material, and choose Two-Color HDPE (Figure 7.3).

FIGURE 7.3   Choose the material you will be using. For this project select Two-Color HDPE from the materials shown.

Step Five

Click on Bit, and select your bit size. For this project, the ⅟₁₆-inch bit is recommended (Figure 7.4).

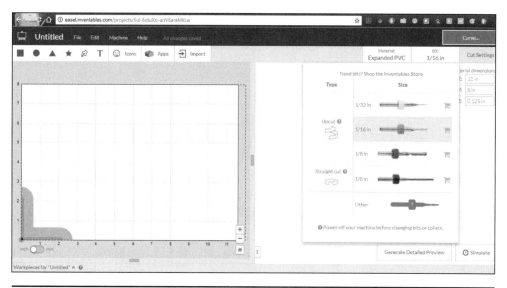

FIGURE 7.4   Select the bit you will use for your project.

Step Six

Change the material dimensions to X = 6 inches, Y = 6 inches, and Z = 0.25 inch. If you are using a different material, be sure to enter the correct dimensions to ensure an accurate carve. You will see that the preview and work areas have now changed to reflect your settings. The settings are important not only for carving your project correctly but also because you will want to preview how your project will carve. Also, if you are carving with a Carvey, a red area will appear in your design space. This represents the clamp that holds down your material in the machine, and you cannot have any of your design in that area. If the settings are not correct, you will not get an accurate preview. Now that you have your workspace set up, you are ready to work on the design!

Step Seven

There are several ways to add elements to your design in Easel.

1.   Click on Icons to open the Design Library (Figure 7.5). Click on the icon you wish to use, and it will be placed in your work area. I selected the umbrella with rain icon.

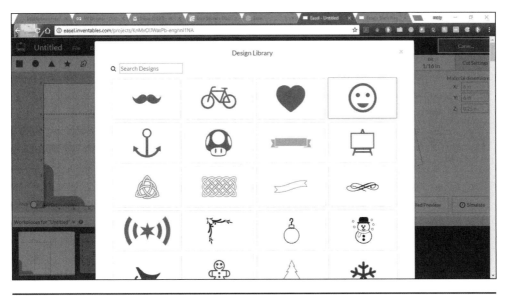

FIGURE 7.5   There are a wide variety of icons to choose from.

2.   One thing you want to keep in mind when designing is how many pieces your complete image will be made up of. As you can see with the umbrella, there are a lot of blue boxes around the various elements of the design (Figure 7.6). These are all individual pieces that make up the larger design.

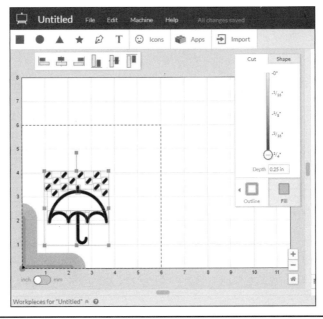

FIGURE 7.6   As you can see, this icon is made up of several different shapes.

If I'm happy with the design as it is, I will want to combine the pieces so that they are one. To do this, click on Edit, and choose Combine. You can now see the entire design as one element (Figure 7.7). Now that they are one element, you can make the entire icon larger or smaller or move it to the area you wish it to be in on your tile.

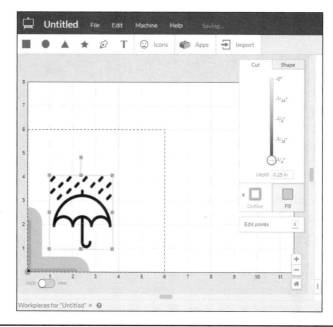

Figure 7.7   You can now see the umbrella icon is one complete shape after using the Combine tool.

3.   Another way to add a design element is to click on Import and select Image Trace (Figure 7.8). Click on Upload to select how you will import a design element. As you can see, there are several options for ways to import a picture, text, and so on to use in your piece. The options include My Computer, Facebook, Google Drive, Instagram, Web Images, Link (URL), and Take Picture. Choose your option, and pick an image to use in your design (Figure 7.9). As you get familiar with the software, you'll find it easier to figure out what kinds of designs work best for different projects. For tiles, simple and bold designs work very well.

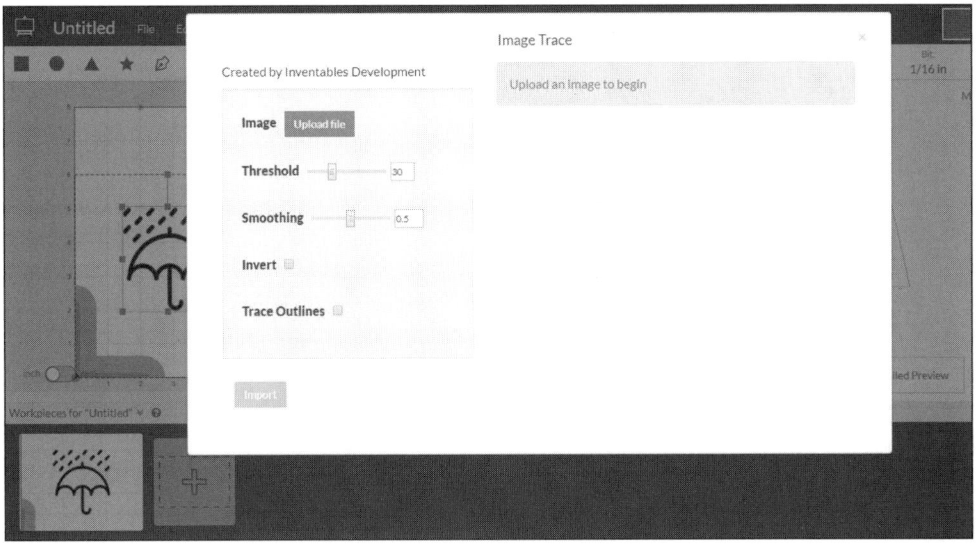

Figure 7.8   Another way to add a design element is by importing a design using the Image Trace tool.

Figure 7.9   You can import an image in a variety of ways.

4.   Now that you have selected a design, you can edit it to your liking in the Image Trace main screen (Figure 7.10). If your image looks okay, you probably don't need to fix the threshold. If the image has a lot of hash marks in it or looks fuzzy, you can adjust the threshold to smooth it out. You may also wish to adjust the Smoothing setting for a better carve. If you push the

Smoothing dial all the way to the right, you will have softer corners, and if you move it all the way to the left, it will make the edges sharper. If you choose Invert by clicking the box, it changes the design so that, in the case of a tile, the background will carve out and the letters will be raised (Figure 7.11). If you only want the outline of a design, you can click the box next to Trace Outlines to have only the outline of the element (Figure 7.12). Once you are happy with your image, click on Import to add it to your design.

FIGURE 7.10   You can make changes to your image before importing to your design space.

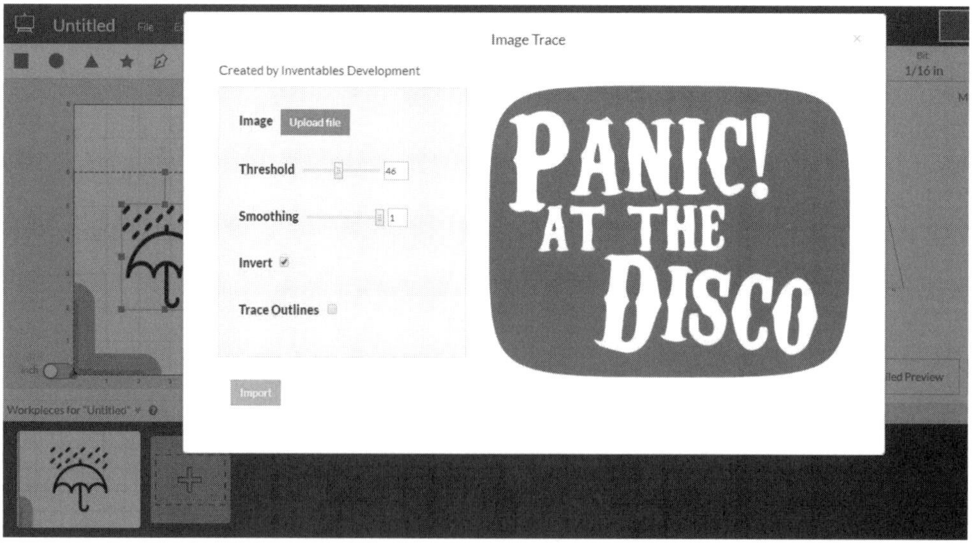

FIGURE 7.11   Inverting the image will change the area that is carved in your final project.

FIGURE 7.12   You can also trace the outline of the image if that is the look you prefer.

5.   You may not want to keep all the words together as one element. To only combine parts of your design, hold the SHIFT key down, and click on the pieces you want to combine into one (Figure 7.13). Click Combine, and those pieces you selected are now combined into one.

FIGURE 7.13   Select the parts of your image you wish to combine.

6. You can add your own text to a design in Easel. To do this, click on the "T" to the left of the Icons tab to open up the selection of fonts (Figure 7.14). Select your font, type in your text, and that's it. The nice thing about using the text feature is that you don't have to worry about each letter being a separate element in the design that needs to be combined. You can now resize your text and place it where you like in your design.

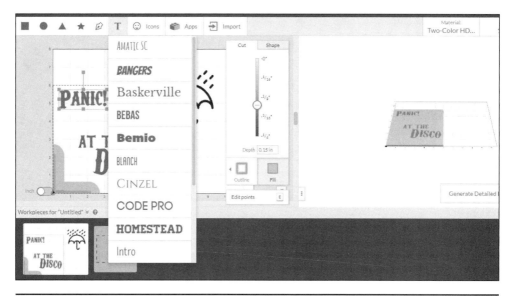

FIGURE 7.14   Add your own text by clicking on the "T" in the menu bar.

7. Lastly, you can add shapes by clicking on the square, circle, triangle, or star.

Step Eight

Now that you have completed your design, you want to set it up so that it carves into the tile deep enough that you can see the color under the top layer but not deep enough that you cut all the way through or see the bottom layer of color. For a 0.25-inch-thick tile, setting the cutting depth at $\frac{1}{16}$ inch to no deeper than $\frac{1}{8}$ inch works best (Figure 7.15). Remember that the deeper you set the depth, the longer it will take for your design to carve out. Click on each element of your design to set the cutting depth. You can always type in the depth in the space provided. Once you have your depths set, click on Simulate in the lower right-hand corner of your preview panel (Figure 7.16). As you can see in the screenshot, most of the design shows up as blue in the preview, but you will notice that the words at the bottom are either orange or you cannot see them. This means that those areas will not carve if you were to send your job to the Carvey as is.

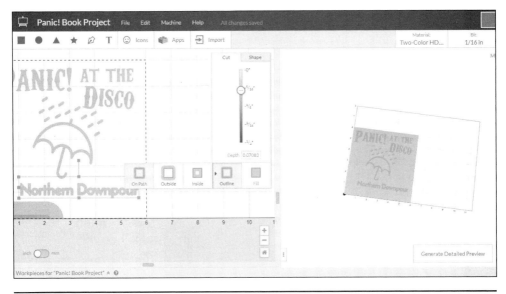

FIGURE 7.15   You need to set the depth for each element of your design so that it carves into the material but not through it.

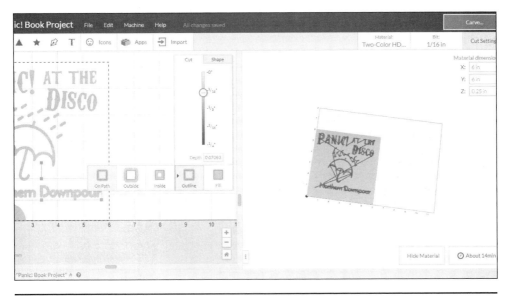

FIGURE 7.16   Click on Simulate to see how your project will carve and how long it will take.

On the Cut panel, you will see Outline and Fill at the bottom. Fill is the default choice, and this option will not carve all of my design. Click on the element of your design that is in orange or not seen in the preview, and then click on Outline. Select each option and Preview each (On Path, Outside, and Inside) to see which option will work with your design (Figure 7.17). Once I have found an option that works, I'm ready to share my design or carve (Figure 7.18).

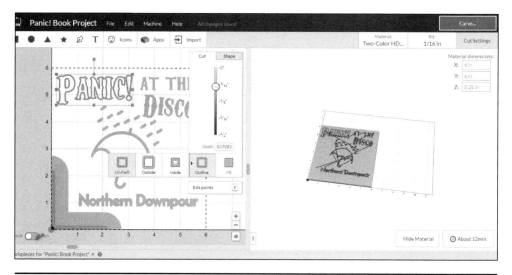

FIGURE 7.17   Check to make sure your design will carve how you would like by experimenting with the Outline & Fill selections.

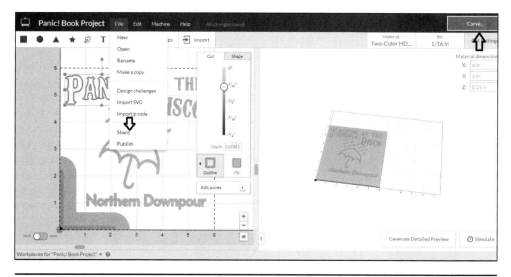

FIGURE 7.18   You can now share and carve your finished design!

Tip: *When working with text or designs that are made up of numerous elements, it's not always an advantage to combine every element. As you can see, depending on the size of the text or style, you may have to choose several different cut settings for the entire design to carve.*

Step Nine

Carve your design! Click on the green Carve button to carve your design on Carvey. You will go through several screens that verify your settings and show you how to secure your material in the machine. When you clicked on Simulate in Step Eight, you should have seen an estimate of how long it would take for your design to carve.

Step Ten

Give your project a name by clicking on Untitled at the top of the screen. You can share your design by clicking on File > Share to generate a URL. You can also publish your design to the Inventables Project's library by clicking on File > Publish. You can upload a photo of your carved design and add a description of your project to share with the Inventables community.

Congratulations! You have completed your first Easel project.

Easel Ornaments

The great thing about a machine like the Carvey is that you can also cut objects out, making it useful for a variety of projects. It's always fun to make customized pieces for yourself, your friends, and family that reflect their tastes and interests. Why not liven up the holidays or your room with a customized ornament!

Ornament from Template

Step One

For this project, we can start out using an ornament template found at www .inventables.com/projects/customizable-ornament-template. Click on Open in Easel to open the template. This will open the template in the Sandbox. You cannot carve or save a design from the sandbox, so click on File > Make a Copy (Figure 7.19).

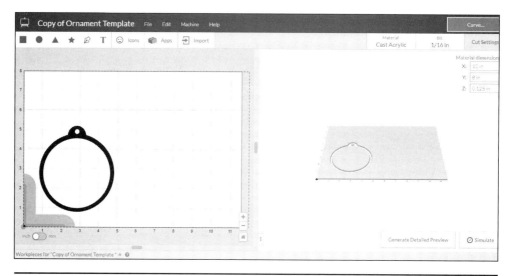

FIGURE 7.19   You can easily make an ornament using the Inventables Ornament template.

Step Two

Change your cut settings to reflect the material and bit size you will be using.

Step Three

Start working on your design using the Image Trace Tool or by selecting from the icons and text features. When designing an ornament such as this, you need to keep in mind that instead of carving into the material, you are cutting the design out, so there are some things to think about.

Not only will your design elements need to be connected to each other in some way, but they also will need to be touching the sides of the ornament template (Figure 7.20).

To add an icon and text, you will want to enter each word of your text individually before combining them so that you can move each letter or number so that it's touching the one next to it. You may need to play around with the fonts or size of the text to get the look you want. For example, Figure 7.21 shows two different fonts and how they look joined together. Once you're happy with how the text looks, combine the letters and numbers and move the image to fit into your overall design. Lastly, combine all your design elements in case you need to change the size of your ornament for carving.

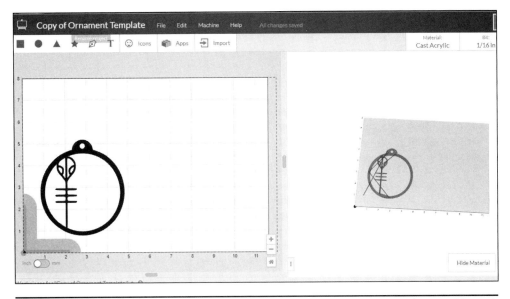

FIGURE 7.20   Your design elements need to touch the sides of the ornament and connect to each other at some point.

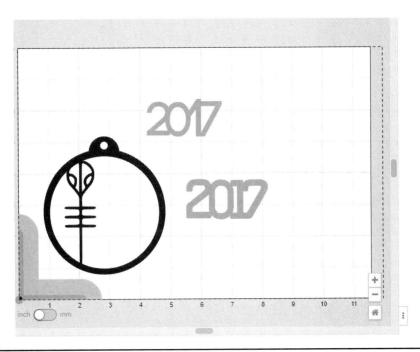

FIGURE 7.21   Test out different fonts to see how they will looked joined together.

Step Four

Once you're happy with the design, there is one more thing that you need to do before you are ready to carve. Because you are cutting out of thinner material, you want to be sure that pieces aren't popping up and getting in the way of the bit while it's trying to carve. If this happens, it can cause the bit to break. Click on your design, and the Cut and Shape toolbar pops up. Click on Outline, and a small box opens up underneath that says Outline/Fill. Select Outside for the Outline setting. Next, check to see if the small box next to Use Tabs has a checkmark in it; if it does not, check this box. Tabs will help to ensure that your design will carve out but leave a small amount of the material in place to hold it all together while it carves. You can move the tabs around by clicking on them and moving your mouse around until they are where you think they will work. You want to be sure that the tabs are in places where they can easily be removed after your project carves (Figure 7.22).

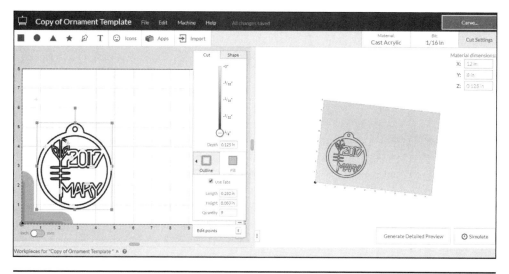

Figure 7.22   You will need to add tabs so your material stays together while carving.

Step Five

Click on Simulate to be sure that your ornament will carve out how you expect it to. You may see bits of orange where you placed your tabs. This is fine because we know that these parts aren't going to carve all the way through (Figure 7.23).

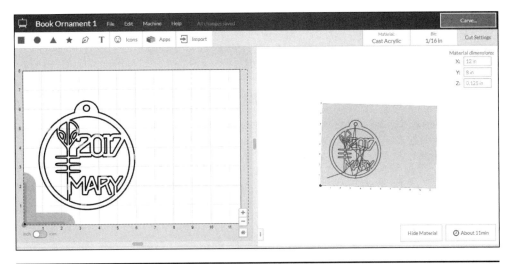

FIGURE 7.23   Click on Simulate to see how your project will carve and how long it will take.

Step Six

Prepare your material for carving by placing a few pieces of removable double-sided tape on the underside of your material. This is an added precaution to hold the material in place. Secure your material to the cutting board with the clamps. Change the bit if you need to, and then close the lid. You are ready to click Carve and carve out your creation.

Free-Form Ornament

For this ornament, you'll create a fast and easy piece using icons.

Step One

Log in to Easel, and open a new project. Change your cut settings as necessary.

Step Two

Pick an icon from the Easel icons, find one on your computer, draw one, or search the Internet and import one via the Image Trace tool (Figure 7.24).

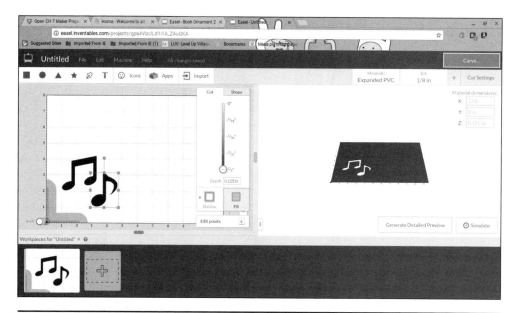

Figure 7.24   Choose an icon or import a design using image trace.

Step Three

Resize your design to the size you wish to it to be. You can play around with the icons you choose by combining them into one piece or just leaving them as is if you prefer (Figure 7.25).

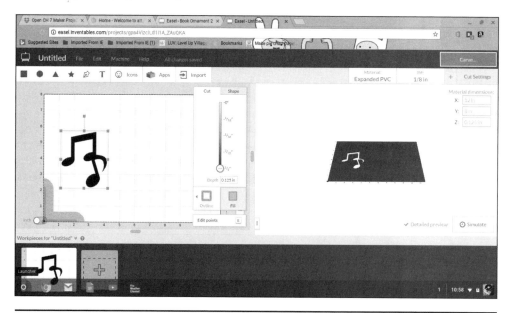

Figure 7.25   You can combine, resize and create the design as you imagine it.

Step Four

To add a hanger to your ornament, click on the circle at the top of the page. This will add a gray circle to your workspace. Resize and move the circle to the part of the design that you think would be a good place to add some ribbon or string by which to hang it. Select the circle you just added and your icon, and then click Combine to make them one piece (Figure 7.26). Click on the circle icon once more to make the inner part of the hanger. Resize the circle to fit inside the first circle so that it will create the hole that you can use to hang the ornament. Do not combine this circle with the rest of your design (Figure 7.27). Next, click Outline, and change the cut depth to the depth needed to cut through your material. Simulate your carve to make sure that it will carve out as you expect (Figure 7.28).

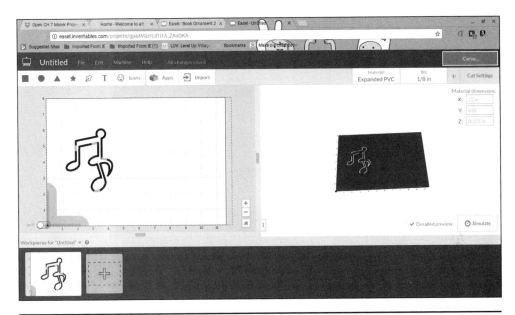

FIGURE 7.26   Use the Circle shape tool to create the hanger.

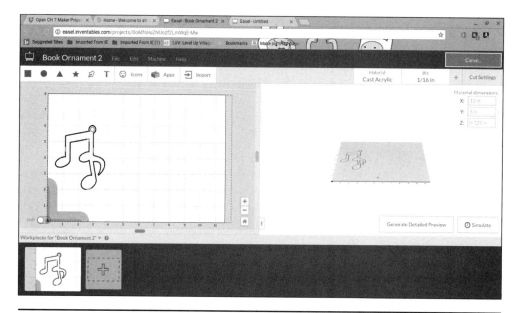

FIGURE 7.27 You will add a second, smaller circle to create the hole to hang your ornament.

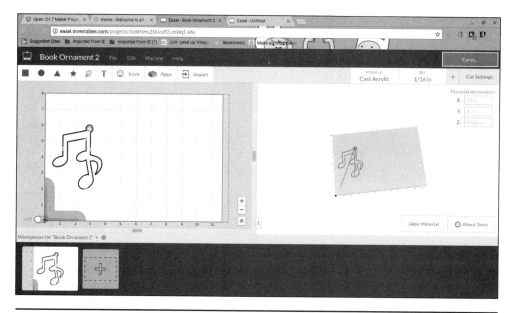

FIGURE 7.28 Again, you will want to simulate your design to be sure it will carve correctly.

Step Five

You are ready to carve your design! Figure 7.29 is a photo of the completed Carvey projects (Inventables, Inc. 2017).

Figure 7.29   These are just a few ideas on how you can create your own unique designs using a 3D carving machine such as Carvey.

DIY Glitter Pins

Pins and buttons are always a fun way to show off your favorite bands and music tastes.

Materials

- Cardstock with real glitter
- T-shirt transfer sheets for ink-jet printer
- Iron
- Parchment paper
- Mod Podge matte waterbase sealer, glue, and finish
- Mod Podge Dimensional Magic

- Paper plate
- Removable foam dots
- Metal back pins or barrettes

Step One

Choose the designs you would like to use for your pins, and create a document in Paint or some other program that will allow you to save and print your sheet. You can also use a royalty-free image site to find some designs you like such as Dreamstime (www.dreamstime.com).

Step Two

Print your designs onto the t-shirt transfer paper. You do not need to reverse the image as you would if you were creating a design for a t-shirt, tote bag, and so on.

Step Three

Cut your cardstock into a smaller piece, and cut out the designs that you will be using. You can cut the designs however you wish, either exactly around the design or leaving a bit of an edge (Figure 7.30).

Figure 7.30   Cut out your cardstock and designs.

Step Four

Carefully peel the backing off the designs you cut out of the transfer paper. Place them on your cardstock (Figure 7.31).

Figure 7.31   Peel the backing off the transfer paper.

Step Five

Place a piece of parchment paper over your design and cardstock, and use a hot iron without steam to iron the designs onto the cardstock. You will see the glitter show through your designs (Figure 7.32).

Figure 7.32   Use a hot iron to attach your designs to the cardstock.

Step Six

Place the designs on a paper plate, and brush a layer of Mod Podge over each one. This will seal the design (Figure 7.33). Let your designs dry about 15 to 20 minutes before moving to the next step.

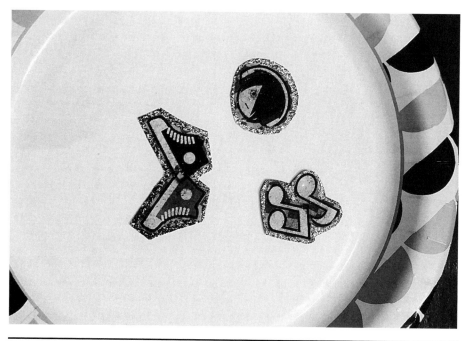

FIGURE 7.33 Brush on Mod Podge and let dry.

Step Seven

Apply the Mod Podge Dimensional Magic by slowly dripping it onto your cut-out designs. It works best to start from the edge and work your way to the center of each piece (Figure 7.34). Be sure not to shake the Dimensional Magic; otherwise, you may find it creating bubbles as you apply it to your pieces. Let the pieces dry for three hours. The product goes on cloudy but will dry clear (Figure 7.35).

FIGURE 7.34   Start from the edges and work your way inside with the Dimensional Magic.

FIGURE 7.35   The Dimensional Magic will dry clear.

Step Eight

Remove your dried designs from the plate, and attach them to the pins or barrettes. Figure 7.36 shows the completed pins (Bulatova 2017).

Figure 7.36   Wear your unique designs on a sweater, on a lanyard or wherever you wish!

Light-Up Tote Bag

Creating a personalized tote bag that not only pays homage to your favorite band but also lights up is a great way to show off your fandom!

Materials

- Transfer sheets for light or dark fabric depending on the color of your bag
- Ink-jet printer
- Fabric tote bag
- Fabric or tacky glue
- LilyPad LEDs in colors of your choice
- LilyTiny or LilyTwinkle (optional)
- Sewable switched battery holder
- Conductive thread

Step One

Find or create an image for your bag. Once you have your file, you will need to reverse the image for transferring to your bag. Use an image editor such as PIXLR (www.pixlr.com/express) to rotate your image so that any text is reversed. You can also use the photo viewer that comes with your computer. This usually allows you to make basic edits, such as rotating, cropping, and adding filters to your photos. Save your image (Figure 7.37) (Eriksson 2017).

Figure 7.37   You will need to reverse your design before printing on transfer paper.

Step Two

Print your design using an ink-jet printer. The transfer paper will not work with laser-jet printers. Follow the instructions that came with your transfer paper when printing. For Jolee's Easy Image paper, you will print your design on the nonglossy side of the paper.

Step Three

Trim the excess transfer paper from your design, and iron the design onto your tote bag. When doing so, use your iron's hottest setting, but do not use steam. You will need to press down on the iron using two hands and make sure that you iron over all parts of your design. Wait for the design to be completely cooled, and start removing the backing from the transfer (Figure 7.38).

Figure 7.38   Peel the backing off the transfer paper once cool.

You may need to reiron parts of the design as you remove the backing. If you see that a part has bubbles or is not staying on the fabric as you remove the backing, just place the backing back over the design, and iron over that area again. Have patience and be careful as you remove the backing. The area you ironed must be completely cooled before you take the backing off the transfer. You could put a design on one side of the bag or both, it's up to you (Figure 7.39)!

FIGURE 7.39   Your design is now on your bag and you are ready to start sewing.

Step Four

Now that you have your design ironed onto your tote bag, you are ready to add the LED elements. Sketch out your design on a piece of paper before you start sewing to be sure that you can sew your circuits the way you want them. If you printed a test of the design on plain paper, you can use that to sketch out your circuit plan (Figure 7.40).

Figure 7.40   Plan out your circuit design before you start sewing.

Step Five

Place a small dab of glue on the back of your battery holder to help hold it in place while you sew. Using the conductive thread, sew through the (+) positive terminal of the battery holder two to three times, making sure that your thread is touching the edges and the stitches are tight to make a good connection. Sew from the (+) positive terminal of the battery holder to the (+) positive terminal of the LilyTwinkle. Repeat with the (−) negative terminal, sewing to the (+) negative terminal of the LilyTwinkle (Figure 7.41).

If you are only sewing on lights, sew from the (+) positive terminal of your battery holder to each light. At each light, sew in place by coming up and through the hole several times, making sure that your stitches touch the edges on the light. Repeat this from the (−) negative side of the battery holder (Figure 7.42).

FIGURE 7.41 Sew to connect the battery holder to the LilyTwinkle.

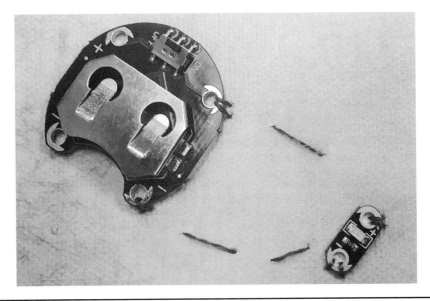

FIGURE 7.42 Sew from the + battery terminal to the + on the LEDs.

Step Six

Sew through the hole at 0, 1, 2, or 3 on the LilyTwinkle or LilyTiny, depending on the effect you wish to have for your lights. You can attach a light from each number or all of them from one of the numbers or whatever combination you like (Figure 7.43).

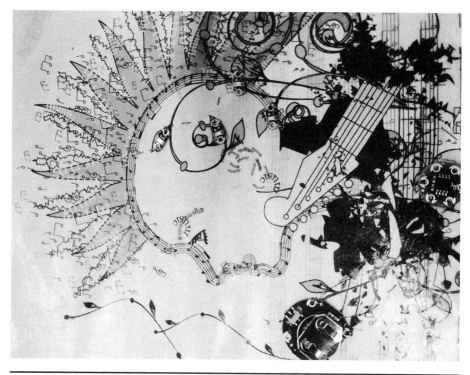

FIGURE 7.43   Sew your LilyTwinkle to the LEDs if adding that element.

NOTE: The LilyTwinkle and LilyTiny are great ways to add some effects inexpensively to your sewable projects. Both are tiny preprogrammed LilyPad boards and are considered an intermediate step in learning how to work with e-textiles. For those of you new to e-textiles or younger, it is often better to leave out the LilyTwinkle or LilyTiny because it adds a bit more complication when planning your design. They are a bit different from each other, so you want to keep a few things in mind when selecting which board is right for your project.

- *LilyTwinkle. This small board is programmed to make your LEDs twinkle and fade. While there are four pins, they have a similar effect, so it's less important which one you sew from.*

- LilyTiny. *This is similar to the LilyTwinkle except that each pin has a different effect: 0 is a steady fade pattern, 1 is a heatbeat pattern, 2 is a blinking pattern, and 3 is a random fade pattern.*

Troubleshooting and Tips

- If your lights are not working, double-check that you have sewn the circuit correctly: negative connections to negative connections and positive connections to positive connections. Also, be sure that you have not crossed your sewing paths and that any loose threads from tying off the end of a stitch are not touching. Both of these things will cause the circuit to short.
- Be aware of the handles of your tote bag when sewing. You may wish to pin the handles down to the top of the bag so you don't accidentally sew through them. Also, make sure that you don't sew through both sides of the bag.
- Make sure that your stitches are not too long and that they are tight. Any loose connections will cause the lights to come on and off.
- You can tie a small knot at the end of your thread so that it doesn't pull through the fabric, but do not tie a knot in the thread to keep it from coming unthreaded while sewing. This makes it difficult to unthread the needle and remove any stitches if you need to fix a mistake (Figures 7.44 and 7.45).

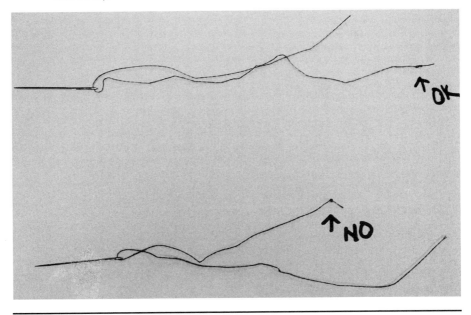

FIGURE 7.44   Don't tie a knot in the piece hanging from the eye of the needle.

FIGURE 7.45   You now have a unique bag that lights up!

Resources

Maker Supplies

Bare Conductive (www.bareconductive.com)

Learn more about the Bare Conductive Touch Board and purchase everything you need to get started with a conductive paint project. Workshop packs are available and ideal for group classes.

Adafruit (www.adafruit.com)

This is one of my go-to sources for maker supplies as well as a great source for ideas and instructions on making all kinds of projects. Bare Conductive, Makey Makey, and e-textile supplies are available here.

SparkFun Electronics (www.sparkfun.com)

This is another great site for project tutorials, learning about electronics, and purchasing supplies to make many of the projects in this book. You can find LilyPad e-textile supplies, the BBC micro:bit, Makey Makey, and more.

Technology Will Save Us (www.techwillsaveus.com)

This company, based in the United Kingdom, specializes in maker kits for kids and teens. Music-based kits include a solderless Synth Kit and a Speaker Kit that is a more advanced project requiring soldering skills. This company is also a great place to find the BBC micro:bit, and the company offers the board by itself or as part of a kit. Find manuals for the kits and project ideas on this site as well.

littleBits (https://littlebits.cc)

This is the place for all your littleBits needs. Purchase the littleBits Korg Synth Kit here as well as other bits to enhance your projects or replace bits you have lost. You can also find project ideas and lessons plans incorporating littleBits on this website.

Music and Recording Gear

Guitar Center (guitarcenter.com)

Visit online or find a nearby store and explore the variety of instruments, DJ gear, microphones, and more. Visiting a music store in person is a great way to get acquainted with music equipment in person. Staff will let you pick up and play an electric guitar or bass, bang on a drum, or try out the synths and keyboards.

Sweetwater Sound (www.sweetwater.com/insync)

You can purchase equipment and instruments here as well as read reviews, check out buyer's guides, and learn some new tips and tricks.

zZounds Music (http://blog.zzounds.com)

zZounds is a retailer similar to Guitar Center and Sweetwater. Check out the company's blog for music news, tips, reviews, and more.

Korg USA (www.korg.com/us)

Learn about all the products and apps offered by Korg. You can find users' guides and FAQs and learn about artists using Korg gear and more.

Learning Music with Ableton (https://learningmusic.ableton.com)

This is a fantastic interactive tutorial that walks you through a variety of music-making techniques.

Books

- *Make: Musical Inventions—DIY Instruments to Toot, Tap, Crank, Strum, Pluck, and Switch On,* by Kathy Ceceri (2017). This book includes a variety of projects where you can learn how to create musical instruments from the simple to more advanced.
- *Getting Started with littleBits: Prototyping and Inventing with Modular Electronics,* by Ayah Bdeir and Matt Richardson. This book is a good introduction to littleBits. It describes the various bits and how they can be used. Chapter 3 covers music and motion and includes a good introduction to synth kits as well as a sample project. This book would be helpful for an instructor to review before the program.
- *The Sound Effects Bible: How to Create and Record Hollywood Style Sound Effects,* by Ric Viers (2008). This is a great book if you are really interested in learning how to create your own sound effects. You will learn everything from how to set up a microphone for a variety of settings to how to create professional sound effects for your projects.

If you are interested in learning more about the history of popular music or perhaps pursuing a career in the music industry, here are some great books for kids and teens:

- *Being a DJ,* by Lisa Regan and Matt Anniss (On the Radar: Awesome Jobs Series).
- *When the Beat Was Born: DJ Kool Herc and the Creation of Hip Hop,* by Laban Carrick Hill.
- *The Story of Techno and Dance Music,* by Matt Anniss (Pop Histories Series).
- *The Story of Punk and Indie,* by Matt Anniss (Pop Histories Series).
- *The Story of Hip-Hop,* by Matt Anniss (Pop Histories Series).
- *Dance Music Manual: Tools, Toys and Techniques,* by Rick Snoman.
- *Electronic Music,* by Nick Collins, Margaret Schedel, and Scott Wilson

Magazines

- *Electronic Musician.* This is a monthly magazine that features articles on musicians, reviews of equipment, advice, and techniques for those interested in creating music using digital and electronic instruments (www.emusician .com).

- *Music Radar Collection.* Home to magazines such as *Computer Music*, *Future Music*, and more. A great resource for exploring a variety of genres and instruments (www.musicradar.com/futuremusic).

- *Recording Musician.* Articles, how-tos, reviews, and more. A great resource for learning more about recording techniques (www.recordingmag.com).

Visit your local music store or book store and peruse the magazine section to find other magazines specific to your musical interests.

Other Resources

- *Lynda.com.* Check your local library to see if it offers a subscription to Lynda.com. This is a great learning resource that includes video classes on everything from GarageBand to Ableton to setting up a studio or learning an instrument! Learning Paths curates a series of Lynda classes into a comprehensive course focused on a particular interest.

  Lynda Learning Paths for Sound and Audio:
  - Become a Music Producer
  - Become a Songwriter
  - Become an EDM Producer
  - Become a Recording Engineer
  - Become a Mixing Engineer

Index

References to figures are in italics.

3D design, 139
    album cover project, 139–151
    DIY glitter pins, 159–164
    free-form ornament design,
        155–159
    light-up tote bag, 164–172
    ornament design from template,
        151–155

A

Ableton, 5, 16
    Learning Music with Ableton,
        174
accelerometer, 128
acoustics, 75–78
Adafruit, 173
album cover design project, 139–151
alternating current, 43
amplifiers, 43
amplitude, exploring with speakers,
    33–43
antenna, 128
apps
    free "lite" versions, 1
    for iPads, 5–7
    recording and editing, 4–5
    See also individual apps
Arduino
    LilyPad Arduino, 7
    software, 8

Audacity, 4, 121
    converting a WAV to MP3, 92–94
    recording littleBits with, 58–62
    storytelling with sound project,
        135–137
Audio Trimmer, 102–105

B

Bare Conductive, 173
Bare Conductive electric paint, 96–97
Bare Conductive Touch Board, 7
    John Henry story board project,
        90–98
    overview, 89–90
Being a DJ (Regan and Anniss), 175
Bluetooth, 128
books, 175
BOSEbuild Speaker Cube, 33
Buechley, Leah, 99

C

Carvey, 139
    album cover design project,
        141–142, 151
compass, 128
condenser microphones, 3
conductive materials, 7–9
conductive mural, creating, 94–97
conductive paint, 96–97
conductive thread. *See* sewing